BEYOND SUPPLY AND DEMAND

BEYOND SUPPLY AND DEMAND

A Reappraisal of Institutional Economics

By JOHN S. GAMBS

GREENWOOD PRESS, PUBLISHERS
WESTPORT, CONNECTICUT

Library of Congress Cataloging in Publication Data

Gambs, John Saké, 1899-
Beyond supply and demand.

Reprint of the 1947 issue of the ed. published by Columbia University Press, New York.
Bibliography: p.
Includes index.
1. Veblen, Thorstein, 1857-1929. 2. Institutional economics. I. Title.
HB99.5.G35 1976 330.1 76-20433
ISBN 0-8371-8993-4

Originally published in 1946 by Columbia University Press, New York

Reprinted with the permission of Columbia University Press

Reprinted in 1976 by Greenwood Press,
a division of Williamhouse-Regency Inc.

Library of Congress Catalog Card Number 76-20433

ISBN 0-8371-8993-4

Printed in the United States of America

To Alice Chase Gambs

"Master, I marvel how the fishes live in the sea."
"Why, as men do a-land: the great ones eat up the little ones." —SHAKESPEARE

THE FOLLOWING persons have, in one way or another, given me generous aid in connection with this book: Leonard Blumgart, Harry J. Carman, Bertha Glotzbach, Allan G. Gruchy, and Wesley C. Mitchell.

My friend Mr. Charles Frederick has given me substantial help on the chapter on methodology, as well as patient toleration. My wife has also given me the latter, and much else besides.

For the ideas expressed herein, I accept full responsibility.

JOHN S. GAMBS

Arlington, Va.
January, 1946

CONTENTS

I GENERAL PRINCIPLES

THIS is a book about the theories of Thorstein Veblen and of other economists who have been inspired by his work. There are several excellent special essays on Veblen and institutional economics, but no well-rounded description and evaluation of what he did and what his followers are trying to do. This little volume attempts to close a gap in economic writing.

Something more than a compulsion to close up gaps has gone into the composing of these pages. During the past ten years much of my energy has been devoted to the practical work of the civil servant, who has played his small role in attempting to plan, install, and administer controls over our economic life in depression, wartime, and now in peace. Out of this experience has come a deeply-felt need, not for better practical schemes or for a multiplication of good programs or ingeniously drawn blueprints, but for a reappraisal of current economic assumptions. This book is a partial outcome of that need. I venture to believe that others may wish to reexamine basic economic issues as an aid in coping with the problems of the day.

The development of radar and automatic missiles, the controlled use of atomic energy, new power constellations in international politics, new power groupings domestically in a dozen important countries—all serve to warn us that the relatively uncomplicated thinking of a decade ago will not save us from disasters even greater than those that have lately befallen us. It is doubtful whether we shall ever again be able to blunder through for a while with NRA's and WPA's and AAA's; whether we can ever again trust the sheer weight of productivity to bring us victory over a strong foe, and whether we can, next time, afford to gamble on the competence of our scientists to bring us first a genuinely effective "secret weapon" like the so-called atomic bomb. This time we shall have to revalue even our fundamentals or take the dire consequences. If we attempt seriously to shape our destiny, we shall have to accept all that science can give us, and if science cannot give us enough, we shall have to call faith or moral law to our aid.

Granted that this is a period of reorientation, why a reappraisal of Veblen and of institutionalism? One reason is that few of his readers are aware of the full implications of his work or of its relevance to the problems of a time like this. Wesley Mitchell has observed that, though many have sipped at the Veblenian spring, few have drunk. His work can stand reconsideration and revaluation. Next, Veblen provides a background against which we can better assess the doctrines of the regnant Anglo-Saxon theorist, John M. Keynes. The books of the British peer, with their promise of full employment and high levels of production, rightly dominate economic thought today. It will give us perspective to look again at an older set of doctrines, to refresh our memories with the salient points of an entirely different type of analysis. A study of Veblen may also suggest that there are other politico-economic questions to ask than the query so frequently made nowadays—oftener in Europe and Asia than in the United States—namely, are you for or against the Soviet Union? Finally, Veblen had a sense of urgency that is appropriate to the mood of the day. In good years and bad, in peace and in war, prosperity and depression, he foresaw great dangers ahead. Though he died before the depression of the thirties, the rise of nazism, and the warfare of the forties, his writings might easily pass as the work of one who has lived through the past twenty years—partly because he foresaw the possibility that the two decades following his death would bring precisely what they have, in fact, brought.

In this country Veblen's ideas have influenced most contemporary economists, and under Roosevelt and even today some of our most highly-placed public servants are said to have been inspired by the dour Norwegian. His best phrases are current coin and have become commonplace in the everyday speech of cultivated people. In recent years, however, Keynes has successfully competed for the interest of the younger men, at least. He promises something that cannot be resisted: full employment and high levels of consumption without serious dislocation of our institutions. Veblen promises the possibility of an even brighter future: a utopian industrial republic—but only alternatively and possibly at great cost. Attainment of the industrial republic requires a dislocation of our accustomed way of life, perhaps sharp conflicts, and exposes us to the possibility of regression towards barbarism.

It would be absurd to say that the future belongs to one of these two great economists, yet something like that is the great issue of the day. The next decade or two will clarify that issue. Those years will probably tell whether the plans of Keynes can be achieved in contradiction to the prophecies of Veblen. They will probably be among the most stirring years of history, and while we may be happy that we are privileged to live through them, we shall be participants as well as spectators, and in either capacity some of us will get hurt.

I do not intend, by these introductory statements, to intimate that this book systematically contrasts the work of Veblen and his followers with that of Keynes—though I shall make occasional references to the latter. Neither shall I be able to point out how institutional theory would amend proposed plans for world reconstruction or what specific program it would sponsor. To discuss institutional theory with some degree of adequacy—if I do that—is a large task. To raise issues and to force, in some minds, a reconsideration of present assumptions, is a sufficiently high goal.

Without further ado, let us begin at the beginning and try to find out what institutionalism is all about. Since there are many misconceptions of institutional theory abroad, these early paragraphs will tell what institutionalism is not. First of all, it is no new and strange mystery completely unrelated to the doctrines of Adam Smith, Ricardo, Mill, and Marshall. Institutionalists accept much that standard economists believe; on the whole they seem to think that what standard theory has to offer is rather elementary and only the beginning of wisdom. Some institutionalists would probably say that their branch of economics bears the same relation to standard or orthodox theory that contemporary physics bears to Newtonian physics. Billiard balls still obey the old laws of motion despite Planck and Bohr, and mud flies off an automobile wheel in conformity with Sir Isaac's theories. But those round objects that click on green baize and seem so solid to the older physicists are, in fact, mostly empty space, and the particles of which they are composed rotate in myriads of galaxies. They do not lie inertly on the table (which is also composed mostly of nothing at all); their sub-microscopic particles pound down, while those of the table pound upwards, in what is actually a precarious equilibrium.

It is, perhaps, impossible to feel much kinship with Newton when you know about X-rays and when you are unable to say whether the primary stuff of a rock is matter or whether it is energy. Similarly, few institutionalists feel much kinship with Ricardo, Jevons, or J. B. Clark. Nevertheless, many of the generalizations of standard economic theory do not conflict with the principles of institutional theory—particularly is this true when one considers that some of the earlier "economic" generalizations of the classicists lay almost as much in the realm of the other biological sciences or of the physical sciences. The institutionalist believes that one can ruin a crop by dumping too much manure on the land, but that small amounts may well be worth a monetary outlay. Too many cooks spoil the broth; ten men in the driver's seat of a truck would be too many, regardless of the economic considerations involved. A moderate tax on rent is shifted with difficulty. Nobody is disposed to object strenuously to the statement that in the long run street-car companies operating with vacant seats tend to make less money per head than companies that pack passengers in like sardines. The consumption of salt if taxed would not go down as much as would the consumption of wine if comparably taxed. All of this is as true in institutional theory as in standard theory.

Institutionalists are willing to go even farther. Although inclined to feel that theories of value are but valuative theories of distribution disguised and reversed, they realize that class-theoretical [1] concepts of value shed less light on economic phenomena than do concepts taking the utility of objects into account. Furthermore, it is to be noted that Wesley Mitchell's work, in various places, has exhibited "a decided kinship with the type of theoretical approach originated by Walras and used at present by Cassel, in so far as they substitute the idea of a multitude of interacting functional relationships for that of single or ultimate 'causes' but Mitchell, of course, does not follow them in focusing attention on the conditions of a theoretical equilibrium in these relationships." [2]

The institutionalist would also accept much that has been done in the past dozen years in the field of monopolistic competition and employment theory—at least to the point of endorsing certain remedial or mitigating measures proposed

[1] This is a term borrowed from the methodological discussions of Brown, *Psychology and the Social Order,* pp. 35 ff. In class theory the behavior or property of objects is determined by the class to which they belong. Thus, Aristotle says that stones fall to the ground, after being thrown, because they belong to the class of ground objects. Before Jevons, theories of value were on this plane of analysis.

[2] Clark, *Preface to Social Economics,* pp. 400–401.

and applauding increased attention to reality. There would, I think, be sharp disagreements on the part of both Veblen and Mitchell with the Keynesian hypotheses.

It is plausible to argue that the static categories of both types of theory are not unlike, but that when standard theory begins to reach out into the realm of dynamics, it parts company with institutional theory, which is essentially a dynamic theory. Perhaps it is plausible, but perhaps it is also nonsense, for one may safely doubt that the concept of static and dynamic categories has ever had any existence in economics except as rhetoric. In any case, it is likely that Veblen, if he were alive, would have felt a moral obligation to reduce Keynes to a cinder.

A Veblenian essay on Keynes would probably have been a caustic document and would have opened with apparent delight that at long last standard theory had extended recognition to and established full diplomatic relations with the business cycle. Of course, he would have reminded the reader, Aftalion and Cassel, Foster and Hansen, Hawtrey and Robertson, to mention but a few, had already given consideration to the matter, but their efforts should probably be considered tentative and somewhat frictional; only now had genuinely cordial relations been established.

He then might have gone on to write an article not too different from one recently written by Otto von Mering.[3] Mr. von Mering attaches great importance to his belief that Keynes's work is adapted to current political and social trends rather than the other way around; Veblen, too, would have noted this and would have aroused suspicions in his reader on this point alone. He would probably have gone much farther than von Mering and would have asserted recklessly that Keynes's chief contribution was that he had devised a formula by which contemporary economists might, while saving most of their doctrines and preconceptions intact, and

3 Von Mering, Otto. "Some Problems of Methodology in Modern Economic Theory," *American Economic Review,* XXXIV, 87–98.

after years of neglect of the business cycle—might, without losing face, now study the long-denied phenomenon of involuntary unemployment.

Veblen would have pointed out, as von Mering points out, that Keynes's choice of constants and variables is arbitrary—that, in other words, some invisible hand had led him to pick out a lucky combination to reach preconceived goals. In this there would have been no questioning of integrity, but rather the suggestion that Keynes, like almost everybody else (except Veblen) is the child of his century—or even decade.

The American's critique in detail might have turned on the optimism with which Keynes seems to feel that speculation can be appreciably reduced and "the proper social purpose" [4] of the market, especially the stock market and similar institutions, restored. Here, Veblen might have said, is normative, classical economic theory unregenerate, still assuming that there are good and bad business transactions and that the good ones have desirable outcomes socially. In any event, the type of criticism applicable to the proposed control of speculation would go for much else in the Keynesian program, namely, that there is a definite incongruity between continuing full employment under peacetime conditions and the spirit of business enterprise. Anglo-Saxon countries will not long be able to keep both.

Finally, and perhaps basically, Veblen would have repudiated the cause-and-effect methodology of the savings-consumption-investment theorists. Man's economic behavior is too complicated to permit of one's being able to pick out a few determinants for a phenomenon as deeply ramified in our lives as is the business cycle. Like Mitchell, Veblen would have said that the problem of the business cycle "concerns the functioning of the whole economy." [5]

Though I have emphasized bases of disagreement in the last page or so, particularly in respect of Keynes, I must re-

[4] Keynes, *The General Theory of Employment, Interest and Money*, p. 159.
[5] Mitchell, "Economic Research and the Needs of the Times," in *Twenty-fourth Annual Report of the National Bureau of Economic Research, Inc.*, p. 37.

turn to the more fundamental observation of an earlier page, namely, that in the broadest sense institutional theory does not and cannot sever all connections with standard theory, or quarrel with all of its propositions, or claim to have a monopoly on all economic truth. Veblen had genuine admiration for the work of Alfred Marshall.

The second thing to note is that there is no one authoritative school of institutional theory. Allied groups or individuals may be distinguished.[6] Contemporary institutionalism has its roots in the work of Sismondi, Richard Jones, Fourier, and Marx. Veblen's work was esteemed by Sombart and Max Weber. In Great Britain, the Webbs, Tawney, John Hobson, and Henry Clay have exhibited characteristics not unlike those of American institutionalists—and have been the teachers of some of them. In this country the greatest names are Thorstein Veblen, Wesley Mitchell, and John R. Commons. It would be invidious to attempt to list others, though perhaps few would object to the inclusion of the name of Robert Hoxie, who died tragically and young, or of Walton Hamilton who inspired the brilliant young men of Amherst during and just after the first World War.

To examine the variety and richness of viewpoints suggested by the names in the last paragraph is beyond the scope of this book, and the reader will have to decide for himself whether I have been wise simply to point out the existence of the many facets of institutional theory, limiting the formal treatment to two categories. The first category will comprise only one name, that of Veblen, because I think his theories, at several crucial points, are quite different from the theories of any of those whose work he has inspired. The latter, however much they may differ from each other, will be unceremoniously placed in the same group, labeled "neo-Veblenians." How to classify Mitchell in this simple taxonomical scheme is something of a problem. He is more Veb-

6 See Harris, "Types of Institutionalism," *Journal of Political Economy,* XL, (Dec., 1932), 721.

lenian than run-of-the-mill neo-Veblenians, yet he does not quite qualify for full-fledged Veblenism. The problem has been met in this book by giving him special handling when his position on the issue under consideration seemed noteworthy.

The neo-Veblenians do not form a distinct group which uses the identifying name of "institutionalist." There is no Institutional Economic Association or Quarterly Review of Institutional Economics. Indeed, institutionalists, though important exceptions may be found, do not like to be typed as institutionalists. Perhaps there was a day when the label would have been a professional encumbrance, but that day has probably passed. The reason is more likely rooted in the fact that the spirit of American scholarship is eclectic and democratic—democratic in the limited sense, at least, that it accepts no doctrinal dictatorships. Much diversity exists. It may be asked whether, in diversity, any positive identification of the institutionalist can be made. We are coming to that, presently; but first let us conclude this section on what institutionalism is not. It is not statistical economics; it is not welfare economics; it is not social criticism. Finally, it is not institutional. This requires clarification. The phrase "institutional economics" was not Veblen's idea. His choice would probably have been "evolutionary economics," as he indicated in one of his most important methodological essays. The currently-used word of identification bears roughly the same sort of relationship to a social institution as the word "romanticism" bears to a *roman.* That is, it is a name at once discreet and noncommittal, certainly related to the word used as base, but pointing to what is secondary rather than primary. This will become clearer as the argument progresses.

We now begin our study on a positive, but still elementary plane, of the more obvious characteristics of institutional theory. Perhaps the one most frequently noted is its breadth of scope. Veblen can scarcely handle the simplest economic problem without discussing its origins in neolithic culture, citing the evidence of the kitchen middens and discussing its probable drift in the calculable future. *Il remonte toujours au déluge.* In the name of the science of wealth he contributes to aesthetic theory and hands us the stone of biology when we seek the bread of economics. We are almost tempted to believe that Pareto must have been thinking of him when he scathingly wrote:

> Here is another marvelous person who wants to substitute psychology for political economy, because many economic phenomena depend on the will of man. Why stop there? Why not substitute geography or even astronomy since, in the last analysis, economic phenomena depend on the seas, the continents, the rivers and especially on the sun, which causes the earth to fructify.
>
> "The womb of earth, supreme and inexhaustible." (V.H.) [7]

Institutionalists have taken economics out of the realm of pseudo-physical science, which is where standard theory seems to want to put it, and have placed it squarely among the biological sciences. They have made—or, at least, valiantly tried to make—its doctrines conformable with those of anthropology, ethnology, psychology, genetics—disciplines that have bothered standard theorists less. They are not much worried by the criticism that their scope is excessive, and they do not take pains to reply to charges. If they did, they would probably say that no science, from astro-physics to zoo-chemistry, is pure; that human knowledge, though fracturable for convenience, is in essence indivisible; that scope is a human invention, unknown to the external world of observable phenomena.

The next thing to notice about institutional theory is that it seems unrounded and incomplete. The really careful reader of Veblen will not have this impression, but anything less than the hardest kind of work leaves the pattern hidden. Mitchell, in a mere chapter of his *Business Cycles,* disarm-

7 V. Pareto, *Traité de sociologie générale,* Paris, Payot, 1932, Vol 1. Translation mine.

ingly discusses something entitled "Economic Organization and Business Cycles." [8] This turns out, in fact, to be a substantial basis for the elaboration of a well-rounded system of economic theory. Something like a system can be disengaged from the work of John Commons. As much cannot be said of other neo-Veblenians, and, in any case, there is no single book to bring together all the leading theories, as is done so well for standard theory in the *Principles* of Marshall, Mill, and Ricardo. Though there are institutionally slanted textbooks, there is no well-graded, neatly-packaged volume named "Elements of Institutional Economics." Neo-Veblenians are addicted in their study to monographs and in their teaching to the discussion of a more or less discrete series of economic problems. They appear to be more often concerned with reform or neo-cameralism than with theoretical considerations.

Most of the above has been by way of superficial introduction to the subject of institutional economics. We come now closer to the heart of the matter and will try to find the genuinely identifying badge of institutionalism. What seems to hold Veblen and his various followers together is an unrecognized premise rather than an overtly acknowledged principle. The institutionalist is always near this hidden premise, sometimes even states it; always "warm" as we might say if economics were a guessing game, accepting unconsciously and preconsciously its force, but rarely dragging it out into the open to have a good look at it, and not often using it explicitly and consistently.

That premise is the one of coercion in economic affairs. "War, commerce and piracy are inseparable," wrote Goethe, and this might well be the motto on some institutionalist device. Mr. Robert Hale, an institutional lawyer rather than an institutional economist, has expressed it in a manner more appropriate to calm reflection:

[8] Mitchell, *Business Cycles; the Problem and Its Setting.* Ch. ii.

All incomes, in last analysis, whether derived from ownership of property or from personal services, are not "products" created by the recipients; they are payments derived from the rest of the community by the exertion of some sort of pressure. To say this is not to condemn the exertion of such pressure; it is the only means a man has, under present arrangements, and perhaps under any workable scheme of things, for keeping alive. . . . The justification of each income must rest on some other ground than that the recipient has "produced" it.[9]

The serenity of Mr. Hale's statement must not be mistaken for the serenity of other Veblenians, who respond with varying degrees of emotional fervor to the existence of economic coercion. Most institutionalists are likely to be quite unscientifically indignant about conflict—and it is doubtful whether they can hide indignation under the devices they have chosen: irony, satire, preoccupation with such "welfare" subjects for study as standards of living or distribution of incomes or unemployment or labor problems. Their mood towards coercion is considerably more agitated than is the mood of the psychologist towards aggression. They tend to feel that certain groups are in a more favorable position to coerce than others; that generally the working class is more coerced than coercing, though no labor-baiter has been more severe in his criticism of the methods of trade unionism than has Veblen.[10] In the main, the institutionalist has assumed that coercion is primarily the rich man's vocation and avocation.

To even the most tolerant and broad-minded institutionalist scientific acceptance of the doctrine of coercion provides no basis for alliance with the Machiavellis, Schopenhauers, Nietzsches, Moscas, and Paretos, who, professing to describe reality, defend some of the most apparently regressive forces of the social world. The institutional viewpoint conveys no implication of approval of an elite, or a superman, or any other class set apart, and sees no virtue in exaggerating human differences. It has no sympathy with von

9 R. G. Tugwell, ed., *The Trend of Economics*, New York, Knopf, 1924, pp. 216–217.

10 Veblen, *Absentee Ownership*, pp. 401–402.

Treitschke's dictum that the "beauty of history" lies in conflict or with von Bernhardi's statement that warfare is a "biological necessity." Finally, by holding out hope for the strengthening of the intelligence and the constructive propensities in man, even the least indignant among the institutionalists would accept Hale's statement as a provisional rather than as an absolute "truth."

Some measure of conflict or coercion has generally been conceded to exist by all economists as an unhappy aspect of economic behavior. Monopoly, unfair competition, exploitation of weaker groups—all are recognized by standard theory. On the whole, however, such phenomena are deemed to be atypical, occasional, and relatively unimportant. Institutional theory erects the occasional into the general. Coercion is deemed to be as pervasive as the air we breathe and, normally, equally unnoticed, except when we are confronted with cruel or shocking or criminal instances of exploitation, monopoly, or unfair competition.

The entire basis of economic theory is changed when coercion, or aggression, instead of competition, becomes the dominant theme of economics. Under the coercion principle the importance to an entrepreneur of properly disposing of scarce goods is minimized and the importance of creating or escaping a coercive situation is maximized. The institutionalist wonders whether the business man really spends much time thinking about a dose of labor *vs.* a dose of capital. Does he not, in the modal case, apportion his resources approximately as his neighbor does, following community practice, rarely going beyond the information available to those who take but a superficial interest in the state of the industrial arts? Does he not, rather, think about such things as how he can maintain independence from his banker or from a larger firm, for which he subcontracts; how he can use patent or copyright laws to secure temporary or quasi-monopoly; how can Jones be appointed as head of the Housing Authority, since Jones is opposed to the building of houses, or

Richard Roe to the Rural Power Commission, since Roe does not believe in electricity? The institutionalist would hold that a business man is less concerned with economic thoughts than with assessing the mood of the community as to where its sympathies lie in respect of a threatened strike; balancing the wisdom of fighting the Labor Relations Commission now against the advantages of waiting until after election; considering the desirability of doing a better job of public relations or the possibility of organizing a share-the-work movement during a period of unemployment in order to head off taxes and large appropriations for relief that would spoil the labor market. Leaders of labor and business and trade-association executives are constantly making noneconomic decisions to achieve economic goals, according to institutional theory. These decisions possibly involve, so far as concern the profits or losses attributable to them, sums whose magnitude considerably exceeds the magnitude of gains and losses growing out of purely economic decisions.[11] If such noneconomic labors as those listed above are successful, scarce goods may be disposed of somewhat haphazardly, the institutionalist would say. If unsuccessful, an economic disposal of scarce goods may be of no avail.

Exchange, the institutionalists might argue, effectuates the trading of equivalents only when the powers behind the exchange are equivalent. The relations of supply and demand remain important, to be sure, not because they determine price, but because they strengthen or weaken one side in the conflict over price.

Those who have not given much thought to the roles of

11 Kenneth E. Boulding makes two statements that are pertinent to the institutionalist view: "a good deal of evidence is accumulating to show that except in times of abnormal instability many, if not most business men, are content to follow rules of thumb in their price and sales policy, without bothering too much about whether a little adjustment here or there would not yield them a larger profit;" and, "a great deal remains to be done in the investigation of actual decisions made by business men . . . the results might be surprising and might necessitate the recasting of a good deal of our analytical machinery." The analytical machinery of standard theory is referred to. *American Economic Review,* XXXII, (Dec., 1942), 802.

force, constraint, and violence in human affairs—and therefore in economic affairs—may be shocked at this emphasis on acts of aggression. Is there any basis at all for the institutionalists' view of pervasively belligerent economic activity? What room is there for fair dealing, honest work, friendly collaboration? The next chapter will develop more fully the concept of human aggression and explain its basis in psychological theory. For the present I can say that certain schools of psychology are also recognizing aggression in activities that formerly were considered under various special and benign instincts—the gathering and collecting instinct, for example. "Conflicts of interest between man and man," Freud says, "are resolved, in principle, by the recourse to violence." [12]

Let it be provisionally assumed that strong traces of hostility and assault may be found in many human activities devoid of even the faintest visible evidence of mayhem or murder. We need not accept Oscar Wilde's hypothesis that all men kill the thing they love, to agree that some men kill it with a kiss.

Interesting corollaries flow from the doctrine of coercion. The first is a denial of the automatic organization of our economic system. In standard theory, as is well known, self-interest expresses itself in the sublimated form of fair competition between peers; this process has the ineluctable effect of employing all who want to work, guiding production, and supplying to each his needs according to his productivity. Standard theory has been revising this chain of hypotheses during the past decade, but it has never been accepted at all by institutionalists or their precursors. Since men practice coercion rather than competition, since great and small power differentials make absence of economic conflicts between political equals the exception rather than the rule, the basic situation premised by standard theory does not exist, and the

12 Einstein, and Freud, *Why War?* p. 26.

consequential organization of our economy is likewise a figment of the mind.

Some degree of organization exists, of course, the institutionalist would have to agree. A certain amount of activity, not entirely unlike the competitive process envisaged by standard theory, does go on, and it provides its measure of organization. Governments add to this by their direction or stimulation or discouragement of certain forms of economic activity, such as in their taxation, tariff, and banking policies. Large business enterprises have their own internal organization and contribute a little towards what orderly arrangement there is. Social institutions have organizing force. They stabilize our wants and probably determine our special methods of production more fundamentally than does the entrepreneur's skill in disposing effectively of capital, labor, and land. Entrepreneurs do not, when initiating action, explore the great universe of possible economic goods or wants or all possible combinations of productive factors. On the contrary: basic building and clothing materials have remained the same for generations, even, in some cases, for millennia; many productive processes and services are the same today as they were in feudal Europe or earlier. Much human activity is safely predictable: men and women marry, have children, get sick, die. Here is a core of behavior to which the community may confidently allot a large fraction of its economically productive efforts in the form of rings, diamonds, diapers, coffins, and the like. Small wonder that some degree of organization can be found even in a coercive economic world.

But there are also disorganization and paradox. There are cyclical business activity and unemployment. The desire to consume basic necessities often can find no way of converting itself into effective demand. American levels of living are highest when the largest portion of our volume of production is being given away to other nations. The wars that free enterprise was to avert have not been averted; or, if one prefers, freedom of enterprise has been averted most successfully on the international plane. Commodities already produced are destroyed to maintain price; natural resources are wasted; agricultural land is "mined," rather than cultivated, and the wholesale economic destruction of erosion and floods is a secondary consequence.

It will be noted that institutional economics here has something like a normative view towards production—the engineer's view. The concept of absolute waste has little standing in orthodox theory; who "mines" his farm land will, soon or late, be overtaken by the inexorable fate that awaits the uneconomic farmer; he will, in the long run (if other things are equal), be outstripped by his competitors and will cease to be an uneconomic farmer. The institutionalist sees no such automatic outcome and has something like an engineer's attitude towards production. Thus, though founded in the physical sciences, his attitude appears to be valuative.

We find that institutionalist writing, in response to the sense of disorganization, has had much to say on business cycles and unemployment and on palliatives for both, such as public works and social insurance. Incidentally, perhaps one reason for the espousal by many neo-Veblenians of schemes for reform is that they have never felt, as standard theorists have, that the clumsy hand of human intervention could disturb the finer workings of the invisible hand. A reform adopted is a way of supplying a measure of order to a system that is characterized by disorder. If there is unemployment, for example, the first choice of the economist is either to counsel a policy of drift or of positive action. If drift is the policy adopted, a conscious choice has been made, based presumably, upon some sort of ethical standard. If the choice takes the form of positive action, ethical standards have also been invoked. In either case, human values enter into the decision. Thus, the institutionalist would say, considerations of welfare or ill-fare have not been gratuitously injected into the situation, but forced into it by economic disorganization.

The second corollary flowing from the basic concept of coercion is the role of money in economic life. Standard theorists hold that money is incidentally, to use Mill's language, a "unit of calculation" and essentially a "mere contrivance for facilitating exchange." [13] To them the value of money is governed by the same laws that govern the value of ordinary commodities. The only difference, Mill says, is that thinking about money engenders confusion and illusion "in minds not scientifically instructed"; discussions of money are therefore often a "mass of vapoury and baseless speculation."

Institutional theory cannot deny that money provides us with a useful unit of calculation or that it facilitates buying and selling. But money is also much more than that. Possession of it is a goal of economic endeavor even after the demand for goods and services and reasonable security has been satisfied. It facilitates not only buying and selling but also buying cheap and selling dear. The very fact that discussions of money are often a "mass of vapoury and baseless speculation" makes possible obfuscations that may be made advantageous to some persons and disadvantageous to others. Since money is (with unimportant exceptions) the only credential required for consumption, no procedure exists whereby the market can distinguish between producers and nonproducers. There can therefore be no guarantee that productivity is rewarded. Man's behavior in respect of using and handling and "making" money is varied, irrational, complicated, and often confused—confused as dreams or primitive magic are full of confusion. This faltering and uncertain behavior is probably a contributing cause of the business cycle—a phenomenon confined to pecuniary economies.

In short, to the institutionalist, money is the nucleus around which cluster infinitely complex forms of human behavior. It is, indeed, a useful unit for reckoning and also the lubricant of sale and purchase; it is, besides, a weapon of attenuated economic coercion. In the monetary economy

[13] J. S. Mill, *Principles of Political Economy,* Bk. III, ch. vii.

"fighting with the mailed fist is prohibited whereas fighting with pounds and pence is sanctioned." [14]

The third corollary is the distinction made by institutionalists between pecuniary and industrial employments. Obviously human beings cannot hope to enjoy long life if their economic activities are limited to general, mutual, and reciprocal coercion. A large part of human effort must go into production. Now, it may be that all persons, in getting their living, make use of their productive as well as their coercive gifts, but some persons and vocations are so completely developed in one or the other direction that a useful distinction can be made between aggressive economic endeavor and productive economic effort. Veblen's phrases are "pecuniary pursuits" and "industrial pursuits." The first is applicable to those who "make" money; the second to those who make goods or supply services of direct social benefit. Standard theory draws no such distinction, because the imputed integrating and organizing function of the moneymaker is considered to be, at least in its ultimate repercussions, a socially useful (productive) effort of high importance—exceptions always being made for such moneymakers as professional gamblers, *rastaquouères,* and the like.

This does not mean that Veblen would deny the industrial or productive role of some moneymakers. The entrepreneur in direct contact with his factory would be exercising both industrial and pecuniary functions—industrial in so far as his knowledge of the industrial arts and his skill in combining energy and matter lead to economical production; pecuniary in so far as he determines advertising policy, price policy, and other broad policies relating to finance, public relations, cartel relations, integrity of merchandise. Presumably the captain of finance—whom Veblen perversely designates as the captain of industry—has no appreciable indus-

[14] G. Mosca, *The Ruling Class,* New York, McGraw-Hill, 1939, p. 57. Mosca was, of course, not an institutionalist, though he, too, gives a central place to coercion in human affairs.

trial function.[15] This is not easy for anyone but the most ardent Veblenian to accept, since the absentee owner, unless he is only a small and passive stockholder, must at least select and delegate a person to assume the industrial functions, supervise that employee somehow, or get rid of him if he is ineffective. Delegation of function is not extinction of function. Despite this objection, Veblen has a point that, even if wrong, is neither frivolous nor heedless of all the facts, namely, that the activities of moneymakers are not necessarily exercised in the interest of production and may often be opposed to that interest.

In his essay on pecuniary and industrial employments[16] Veblen suggests many things that receive further development elsewhere in his books or have been developed by his followers. One concerns the fitting of goods for sale (pecuniary concern) rather than use (industrial concern).[17] A straight line could almost be drawn from that sentence in his essay, through the early work of Stuart Chase, to the latest reports of consumers' advisory services. Veblen apparently believed —indeed, it seemed to be axiomatic to him—that commodities which did not completely and exactly fulfill the functions essential to their nature had been perverted by some sinister force, such as an evil social institution, or a pecuniary contamination, or misplaced faith in magic, or the animistic preconceptions that dominate the barbaric mind. His book *The Theory of the Leisure Class* derives some of its widely-appreciated humor from his citing of the grave discrepancies between the essential function of a commodity and the perverted function (e.g., women's shoes: essential function to protect the feet and facilitate walking; actual and perverted function, to deform the feet and inhibit walking). Here, again, in the field of consumption, as in the field of production, we find the engineering attitude—stretching the meaning of that phrase to cover also the attitudes of the physician,

15 Veblen, *The Place of Science in Modern Civilization,* p. 292.
16 *Ibid.,* pp. 279–324.
17 *Ibid.,* p. 298.

nutritionist, and others concerned with the applications of the nonsocial sciences to human purposes.

This same essay also points out that the two types of employment, pecuniary and industrial, are more than mere matters of vocation. Each is a way of life; each breeds in its practitioner special and antagonistic ways of thinking and doing. In a society like ours, where the machine is becoming ever more complex and pecuniary transactions multiply, a chasm of differing beliefs and aims already separates the two groups, and misunderstanding threatens to increase. This neo-Marxism is supported, as we shall see, by a brand of psychological theory in which deuces are wild and the stage is set for a possible struggle between the classes.

Analysis and appraisal of Veblen's pecuniary-industrial thesis will run through the next two chapters. At this point a few preliminary observations are timely. First, most neo-Veblenians do not accept the strict and literal dichotomy. Wesley C. Mitchell does employ the basic concept, that the imperious need of businessmen is to make money (profits), not to make goods or render services of social worth. Because they can perform this function, they are permitted to lead the industrial army, despite the fact that industry, operating under the profit limitation, becomes the victim of cyclical and other debilitating influences.[18] Secondly, recognition of the two types of activity explains certain otherwise curious or paradoxical phenomena, such as profitable bankruptcies and the dominating role of advertising in economic life. It also facilitates clarification of the concept of social cost *vs.* costs to the individual entrepreneur; John M. Clark's study of overhead costs is considered a leading work in this field as well as in the field of business cycles.[19] Finally, it may be pointed out here that if Veblen has made a contribution on this point, his ideas seem to need refinement. Other descrip-

18 Mitchell, *Business Cycles*, ch. ii.

19 J. M. Clark, *Studies in the Economics of Overhead Costs*, Chicago, University of Chicago Press, 1923.

tive words seem to be needed. The word "political," in a special sense, might be better than either "pecuniary" or "coercive," but would probably be confusing. The intention would be to distinguish between those whose title to consume is gained by the manipulation of human beings and their emotions and those whose title is acquired by the manipulation of matter. But this would not work; professional dancing, for example, though intended for the second category, is covered by the first. Tawney's "acquisitive" seems better, but not quite good enough.[20] It must already be clear that one distinction between standard and institutional theory is that the former relates primarily to issues of distribution, the latter to the process of acquisition.

The last corollary to be noted here revolves on the importance of the evolutionary or institutional "approach." Veblen's constant awareness of changing institutional life was an important ingredient of what he named "evolutionary economics," and "evolutionary" was what he himself thought was distinctive about his economic writing.

In this he was partly right, in that a strong utopian bias was a dominant trait in his make-up, and his theories held out the possibility of far-reaching social changes through changing institutions; this in part distinguished his work from that of standard theory. But he was also partly wrong, for as an economist, rather than as a prophet or dreamer—as a mere economist—his acceptance of coercion as a basic means of acquiring wealth was his really grand theme.

Institutions, in the Veblenian system, tend to give a semi-permanent coercive advantage to certain groups at the expense of others. A study of cultures in time and space, reveals that semi-permanent coercive advantages may fall to quite different groups. In some tribes men have all the advantages, in others women; warriors in this culture, priests in that one; landlords here, shopkeepers there. As any culture

20 Tawney, *The Acquisitive Society*.

changes, the advantages of one group may count for little in a new environment, while formerly submerged groups may rise to the top of the scale of coercive power.

The nature of coercive power differs from institutional system to institutional system, and probably varies in complexity directly with the complexity of the culture. The fact that a persistent coercive advantage is useful in the acquisition of goods and services, endows the advantage itself with something akin to economic value, and sets men who do not possess the advantage to thinking how they can acquire it—or negative the advantage possessed by others, or acquire a superior advantage. In short, men strive to create new rights, or to alter existing institutions or legislation because of the economic advantage involved.

An awareness of the capacity of institutions to change is an awareness that the rules of the economic game may be changed. This circumstance may often alter the ground of economic conflict, from a conflict over things to a conflict over proposed or presently existing arrangements. Mr. Walton Hamilton has a good example:

> In the pecuniary calculus the lasting costs of a strike—in impaired morale, in disorganized labor force, in a cataclysmic break in activity—are discounted to almost nothing; and the insistent demands of the workers are exalted almost to treason against the established order. In such matters wages and hours are held of less account than the inroad upon an indefeasible managerial authority.[21]

Economic conflicts thus take place on the political field as well as in the market place. When unemployed millions refuse the economic way of finding jobs—deflation of wages and reduction of standards of work—and take instead the political way, institutions may be changed, and we find that politics may determine economics. That is an important discovery. It means, for one thing, that human beings are not, as standard theory often suggests, guided by a sort of eco-

[21] H. E. Stearns, ed. *America Now,* New York, Scribners, 1938, p. 157.

nomic imperative; human beings turn to any means at hand to make a living. There is no innate human propensity to develop or safeguard or use an economic system based on free exchange to obtain scarce goods. The innate human propensity is to take—and sometimes to make—but not to truck and barter on a basis of equivalence. As a result, economic arrangements are constantly being altered by a world of laws and practices that standard theory frowns upon.

It is worth observing in this connection that standard economic theory assumes a perverse tendency on the part of government to interfere in economic affairs. Institutional theory holds otherwise: first, that groups organized for pecuniary gain urge or coerce governments to interfere for their benefit in economic life; second, that the economic organization of society, being imperfect, perennially requires that government step in to remedy the deficiencies caused by the forces of economic disintegration and to minimize the social and political repercussions of economic disorganization; third, that various phenomena, of which war is one of the most conspicuous, cause a shift in scales of valuation, leading "with startling suddenness to a drastic change in economic organization," [22] a shift which leads to intervention and, in the ordinary course of events, to a consequent institutional change.

We come now to a second fundamental principle of institutionalism; it concerns method rather than content. Like the coercive principle, it is accepted only tacitly and unconsciously by most of the neo-Veblenians, and often inconsistently. It is hard to describe; I do not expect to do justice to it in the next few paragraphs. The third chapter, on methodology, will, I hope, make up for the unavoidable deficiencies of this preview.

The principle may provisionally be named the "doctrine of organic unity." It can be partially explained by using the

22 W. C. Mitchell, *Wartime 'Prosperity' and the Future,* New York, National Bureau of Economic Research, 1943, p. 3.

word Gestalt in its special psychological sense, though the word was not current in Veblen's day and was not used by him. Gestalt theory holds, roughly, that wholes determine parts; that wholes are not mere summations of parts; that there is a certain harmony or congruence between the whole and the part. The principle affirms that individual behavior, economic action, and social behavior move together, like three billiard balls in a bowl—as Marshall said about something else. Move one, and the other two must move with it. Hold one still, and the others will not budge.

The same dominating force in a Gestalt which determines that our economy shall be coercive-pecuniary-mechanical also shapes our habits of consumption, our religion, our manners, our attitudes towards birth, love, death, and God. In its practical applications this principle, especially in debased form, may often make the institutionalist seem to be a simple-minded economic determinist. More skillfully used, it is an interesting analytical tool. Mitchell uses it to good effect in his studies of business cycles, which hold, as a fundamental principle, that such cycles are phenomena completely and inescapably bound up with the pecuniary economy.

It is admitted that today's Gestalt may contain left-over elements from yesterday's Gestalt. Thus, there can be culture lags, and these culture lags may be of great significance. Veblen pointed out several decades ago that the Germans and Japanese could be expected to disturb the peace, because their Gestalts were characterized by excessive incongruities. He pointed to the danger of placing modern industrial machinery in the hands of nations still dominated by feudal concepts.

Perhaps the principle of organic unity has its greatest immediate usefulness in appraising the feasibility of schemes for what is known as world reconstruction, full employment, or the management of mixed economies, such as are being planned in western Europe. It would give a cue for reply to the question as to whether our American Gestalt is one that would tolerate the maintenance of high levels of employment in conformity with the Keynesian hypotheses (assuming they have validity). It is not within the scope of this book to reply to that question, but I think Veblen would have said "no." This, taken by itself, is no reflection on the worth of the goal or on the logical validity of the Keynesian doctrines. The issue is simply whether the solutions envisaged fit the current Gestalt.

The fundamentals of institutional theory have now been given sufficiently and in enough detail to furnish perspective for what follows. It has been an exercise in self-discipline not to include more: Veblen's American economic history, for example. But this book is not about Veblen or even, in the usual sense, about institutional economics. It is a re-appraisal of the theories of institutional economics.

The next chapters will return to the principles discussed above, but not by the procedure of increasingly intensive consideration of the same material. Instead, we shall look at some of the basic assumptions and preconceptions by which Veblen and other institutionalists have arrived at their principles. These we shall attempt to understand and to evaluate. The conclusions we reach in our appraisal of the basic assumptions—whether consciously made or accepted unconsciously—those conclusions will determine the extent of our agreement with the principles set forth above.

This, incidentally, was Veblen's method of appraising standard theory. His analysis rarely went to the actual ideas put forward by Ricardo, Jevons, and Marshall; it went to the underlying assumptions and preconceptions. Let us now look below the surface of institutional theory, to see what hidden premises we can find.

II PSYCHOLOGY

WHY do institutionalists talk so much about psychology? Can one not be a good economist without being also an amateur reflexologist or psychoanalyst? In the past ten or fifteen years the best efforts of standard theory have gone into studies of imperfect competition and full employment. What light can John B. Watson or Sigmund Freud throw on these topics? Lionel Robbins has asked himself almost exactly the same questions and has concluded that those who devote much attention to the relation of psychology to the science of wealth are men who "have been ignorant of Economics, but anxious, for various reasons, to discredit its conclusions." He adds darkly that "people who have worried much about such matters have had other ends in view." [1] It is certainly true that institutional economists are indifferent as to whether their work discredits the theories of standard economics, but this is not the same thing as wishing to discredit the great, wide field of serious and conscientious economic study—a field in which Mr. Robbins occupies a small though distinguished place.

Mr. Robbins and others are probably correct, however, in stating that psychology offers few if any direct and constructive replies to certain questions of great interest to standard economics and to the world of practical affairs. In the science of wealth psychology has an important initial function, a function that diminishes in utility as the science is elaborated. Psychology is like the foundation of a house. The importance of a foundation in a building is undisputed, but when the

1 L. Robbins, *The Manchester School,* V (1934), 89.

whole is completed, the supporting masonry is often invisible, unadmired, undiscussed, and unmentioned. It plays forever a determining role, however. It limits the size, shape, and use of the structure above—octagonal skyscrapers are not built on what was intended to support a small rectangular dwelling. Despite its determining character, moreover, a foundation may provide no basis whatever for answering certain types of questions: whether heat shall be by hot water or steam; where to build the verandah; what roofing materials to use. The concepts of imperfect competition and of the savings-investment analysis are rooted in standard theory. The psychological considerations appropriate to the foundations of institutional theory may have no direct relevance to problems arising in some other system of thought. The Keynesians, to take an example, would probably test the value of an economic psychologist by ascertaining whether or not he could make fruitful inquiries into the expectations of entrepreneurs—fruitful inquiries into the propensity to consume having already been made without much use of psychology. It is doubtful whether a Veblenian could, in the same vein, add much to the famous Chapter XII of the *General Theory*.[2] He would probably have to disagree so completely with so many of the other chapters of the *General Theory* that there would be no contact at the twelfth station. It would be like the chemist attempting to answer the questions of the alchemist—or vice versa if the reader prefers.

A proper approach to the question of how institutional theory and psychology are related begins with a realization that institutionalists still think of their science as being in the foundations stage. The institutionalist thinks of himself as the practitioner of a young rather than a perfected mystery. On the 175th anniversary of Columbia University, Wesley Mitchell made an address entitled "Economics, 1904–1929." [3] His first sentence was: "Whether we call Adam Smith

2 Keynes, *The General Theory of Employment, Interest and Money*, ch. xii.
3 Reprinted in his *The Backward Art of Spending Money and Other Essays*.

or François Quesnay the 'father of political economy,' the science is younger than Columbia University." This sentence was more than a graceful opening. It expressed the institutional view that economics is young and immature. Veblen wrote that the economic life process was "still in great measure awaiting theoretical formulation," and this is quoted on the fly page of C. E. Ayres's recent book on institutional economics.[4]

In this stage a science must familiarize itself with its universe and the prospects of that universe. It cannot give pat answers to Mr. Chamberlin, Mrs. Robinson, or Mr. Keynes. In this stage psychology is important. Perhaps it should be noted that when Jevons derailed the car of economic science, he used psychology as his lever. This metaphor is a way of saying that standard theory, too, at a time when it was radically overhauling its structure, developed a strong interest in psychology.

Institutionalism has already come to certain definite conclusions about psychology and economics. The first is that all economists use psychology, consciously or unconsciously, even when they are opposed to its use. This thesis has been competently defended.[5] A second is that economic behavior is but a special form of behavior and therefore can be understood only if behavior in general is understood. Institutionalists therefore ask whether economics should not dwell with the biological sciences, instead of inhabiting some Shangri-la under the alleged governance of the physical sciences—which is where standard theory seems to have its being.[6] If this ques-

[4] Ayres, *The Theory of Economic Progress.*

[5] See Mitchell, *The Backward Art of Spending Money and other Essays, passim,* especially, pp. 177, 361, 369–371, 407–408, and Clark, *Preface to Social Economics,* ch. iv., n.b., p. 96. B. H. Higgins, in *The Manchester School* (Vol. VI, No. 1), discusses an article by L. Robbins on the fruitlessness of the relationship between psychology and economics (*Manchester School,* Vol. V, No. 2). Mr. Higgins shows that the latter makes vast psychological assumptions, even while denying that psychology can play any important role in economic thinking.

[6] Le XVIIIe siècle est encyclopédiste. Les sciences de la nature exerceront sur la formation des idées physiocrates et smithiennes une influence conforme à ses habitudes d'esprit. Ainsi, de science à science, se propagera la "confusion

tion can be answered affirmatively a complete re-orientation of economic study is suggested. The unit of study now is protoplasm rather than prices; the subject is human behavior rather than the behavior of money or a unit of fertilizer or a dose of capital; the mathematics appropriate primarily to nineteenth-century physics are discarded in favor of the mathematics applicable to biology; rent is the income of a person, not the special contribution to production of a piece of land. Concepts relate to process, change, adjustment, rather than to equilibrium, statics, dynamics. To Veblen all this does not mean that economics becomes less nearly exact, or gives up the rigorous ideals of the more nearly exact sciences. Science is science, and if standards of workmanship fall below the highest, they should be improved. But the degree of exactitude possible at any given stage of development is dependent on the nature of the phenomena, not on the family connections claimed for any special science.

In brief, among the questions that institutional economics asks are the early, elementary questions—the ones whose answers are almost the axioms of standard theory. What gives organization—such as it is—to the economic world? Are the concepts of supply and demand useful? Why is work a pain instead of a pleasure? Why is consumption a pleasure instead of a pain—especially the consumption of high heels, corsets, high stiff collars, and similar admittedly uncomfortable contrivances?

Before we go on to the felling of the larger trees, let us clear away some of the underbrush. First, it is worth noting that no type of economic theory stands to gain much from psychological theory if the latter be dragged into the discussion on an inappropriate level. Thus, if an economist is making an historical study of some great migratory movement under the plausible hypothesis that voluntary human migra-

des langues." S. Bauer, "Origine utopique et metaphorique de la théorie du 'laissez faire' et de l'équilibre naturel," *Revue d'economie politique*, 45e année, No. 6, 1931.

tion is normally motivated by a desire for improvement of economic status, it adds little, save elegance, to show that a desire to attain religious liberty motivated a few of the migrants, or that some of the possible migrants stayed home because the ties of motherland and old friends pulled stronger than the lure of wealth. It does no good to keep on insisting, as some institutionalists do, that certain motives in certain people are stronger than economic motives, when the net result is approximately the same as it would have been had economic motivation alone been considered.

On an entirely different level of analysis one might, however, ask pertinent psychological questions. Why did the migrants choose the uncertainties of sea and wind and weather when they might have improved their economic condition at home by political action? Why did they not foresee that the personal risks of political action at home would not be appreciably greater than the risks of migration, in which new settlements were virtually wiped out by disease, famine, cold, and the arrows of the natives? Counting out the very few who had spectacular success, were the new economic conditions superior to the old? To what degree may the concept of sheer gambling on the possibility of economic improvement be identified with the concept of economic self-interest? Did not the migratory movement, at its peak, become entirely irrational, attracting numbers far in excess of what sober estimates of economic opportunity would ever suggest? Does the study of such a migratory movement clarify any phenomena of the business cycle, which sometimes also rises to a crest of frenzied activity? Here we have a series of psychological questions that are appropriate to the inquiry.

Second, it is worth noting that psychological theory, like economic theory, is in the hands of several dissident schools. It soon seems relevant to ask which school is correct. The proper answer is that the question is unconstructive and deserves no direct reply. The world of psychology, like that of economics, is one in which certain hypotheses have been generally abandoned, others provisionally accepted, while still others contend for supremacy. A professional psychologist is one who is reasonably well-informed on the nature and status of these hypotheses. His prejudices may lead him to assume that dubious hypotheses are among the provisionally accepted, and vice versa; but even his prejudices have had to withstand the claims of hypotheses towards which he may still be unsympathetic. The impact of rival theories has given him an understanding of human behavior and motivation that is not possessed by other men. Schools may disagree, but the member of any school is more competent than those who have never thoughtfully considered what the schools have to offer. As economists, we ourselves will discover certain things about human behavior. To clarify our own thinking we call on the contributions of psychology that are helpful. If psychology can give us no help, we invent our own theory—but in that case we must be careful that our theory is at least in rough harmony with the more substantial hypotheses relating to the human psyche. Despite all the disagreements among psychologists, their science, like ours, has reached certain areas of agreement—if only negative ones—at least equivalent, let us say, to the economists' repudiation of the naïve labor-theory of value.

What are the psychological theories of institutionalism, and what light do they throw on economic theory? If we begin with Veblen, we find that his first job was, as the phrase has it, "destructive." He repudiated the kind of psychology that had been used, both consciously and unconsciously, by standard theorists. He attempted to show that the psychology of the then-ascendant economic thinkers was at variance with the then-current psychological theories of James, Dewey, and others. He tried to use, often with success, the theories of his contemporaries and to bend them to the service of his economics. He speaks of instincts after the fashion of his colleagues. Like them he anticipates the behavioristic and pragmatic doctrine that human nature is highly malleable. Veblen is rather contradictory here, since he seems to feel that man's vanity and predatory instinct cannot easily be rooted out—but more of this later. In detail, he makes shrewd, homely observations that most academic psychologists probably would not pay much attention to, for example, that coercion and predation are fun, whereas ordinary work is drudgery. He recognizes the existence of certain spurious human needs—the need to carry a cane, bind the feet, wear rings in the nose. These he would distinguish from functional needs, like mating, or inquiring curiously into the environment. This sort of distinction, as deeply rooted in the imperatives of biology as in those of ethics, sometimes makes him seem to be more nearly a moralist than he really is. In all this he was, with perhaps only minor reservations, acceptable enough to most of his academic colleagues in the departments of psychology. But he went considerably beyond them, into territory which was and still is more doubtful.

His psychological apparatus has both formal, or explicit, and informal, or implicit, elements. The formal elements, as intimated above, are the accepted hypotheses of his day, more or less stretched to suit his needs or his way of thinking. The informal and implicit elements seem to derive from his observation of real people, from the conclusions he reached as the result of his anthropological studies, and from the needs of his economic theory. The latter are among the most interesting part of his psychological equipment. Very often they suggest the work of Freud. This may be surprising, for Veblen apparently knew next to nothing about psychoanalysis. Mr. Dorfman's biography, judging from the index, mentions Freud only once, and that in a subsidiary connection. But if one considers that both Freud and Veblen got some of their ideas from the same sources—from direct observations of human beings, from a study of Darwin and of the legends, magic, animism, and ceremonial of primitive man—it is not too surprising that at some points their theories should come together. Both, moreover, held certain methodological principles in common—something that directed their eyes to similar phenomena.[7]

The opposition of constructive and destructive tendencies is the key to Veblen's work. Just as Bentham opposed pleasure and pain, so Veblen opposed constructive and destructive propensities. Out of this opposition flows a balanced system which combines notions of individual, economic, and social behavior in a vast synthesis. The reader has not far to go in *The Instinct of Workmanship* before he is struck by the interesting trinity: workmanship, parental bent, and idle curiosity. These three instincts were blended into a sort of unified constructive propensity, again reminding one less of James and more of Freud, who postulates a basic reaction tendency, or force, that "impels us to build up, to construct, to preserve ourselves and the species." [8] The Veblenian dichotomy, business and industry, finds a parallel in the Freudian polarity, destructive urges and constructive urges. For the purposes of economics, Veblen abstracts what he most needs from this constructive tendency, ignores love and parental bent, skimps idle curiosity, and becomes very explicit about "industrial pursuits." These are the economically important manifestations of the constructive instincts, particularly the instinct of workmanship.

And now he makes a most remarkable observation. The instinct of workmanship, he says, is capable of contaminating itself. We engage in an industrial pursuit, but tend to contaminate the purely industrial activity by vain ritual, incantation, or superstition. Thus, a farmer will plant (industrial pursuit) by the light of a waxing moon (superstitious contamination). Or there will be a tendency to carry over the inconveniences of a past age into the next age; our buildings of today, for example, reveal unnecessary shortcomings

[7] For a discussion of Freud's methodology see Brown, *Psychology and the Social Order*, pp. 325 ff.

[8] *Ibid.*, p. 308. For Freud's own statement see his *New Introductory Lectures on Psycho-analysis*, pp. 141 ff.

because the fundamental principles of their design were conceived at a time when glass, central heating, principles of ventilation, plumbing, gas, electricity, radio, and telephones were unknown. Though we expend genuine constructive propensities in whatever we do, the result is a mixed product which also betrays a sort of destructive instinct or a perverted ("contaminated") instinct of workmanship.

Veblen realizes how incredulous the reader must be and inserts the following into the text:

> A doubt may plausibly suggest itself as to the competency of such an explanation of these phenomena. It would seem scarcely to lie in the nature of an instinct of workmanship to enlist the workman in the acquisition of knowledge which he cannot use, and guide him in elaborating it into a system which will defeat his own ends; to build up obstructions to its own working, and yet in the long run to overcome them. In part this discrepancy in the outcome arises from the fact that the sense of workmanship affords a norm of systematisation for the facts that come into knowledge. This leads to something like a dramatisation of the facts, whereby they fall into some sort of a sequence of conduct among themselves, become personalised, are conceived as gifted with discrimination, inclinations, preferences and initiative; and in so far as the facts are conceived to be involved in immaterial or hyperphysical relations of this character they cannot effectually be made use of for the purposes of technology. All conceptions that exceed the scope of material fact are useless for technology, and in so far as such conceptions are intruded into the body of information drawn on by the workman they become obstructive.[9]

The phrase "and yet in the long run to overcome them" (second sentence of quotation) seems to refer to the fact that in due course of time workmanship abandons its vain ritual, or traditionalism, or animism, and a genuine functionalism dominates. Thus, the concept of a horseless carriage dies after awhile, and we become at last genuinely "automobile-minded." Our capacity to do this he ascribes to idle curiosity, an instinct that seems to be the force behind theoretical discovery in science.

[9] Veblen, *The Instinct of Workmanship*, pp. 84, 85.

Veblen is not too clear about some of his ideas under these headings—and it is interesting to note that Freud, at least in his earlier work, is rather weak at the same point—but it seems safe to say that Veblen assimilates the contaminated instinct to coercion, aggression, warlike propensities, predation, effrontery—and, for the present stage of human development, to the motives underlying pecuniary pursuits.

We may restate the Veblenian position, then, by saying that men at this historical juncture are pursuing two types of economic activity: constructive or industrial and pecuniary, or aggressive and coercive. In all this, it will be noted, Veblen does not rely, as James did, on a host of special instincts (like that of licking sugar!). There is, in fact, only one instinct—and its contaminated part. We have, indeed, polarity and monism rather than dichotomy and pluralism. Workmanship leads to animism; animism invites a congeries of destructive tendencies.

Veblen traces the development and manifestations of the instinct of workmanship through the ages and holds that each stage of development seemed to call forth an appropriate contamination. Early workmanship evoked notions of animism; it apparently was repressed in the Middle Ages, and this repression presumably had something to do with the warlike character (contamination) of the period; in the handicraft era God became the Great Artificer and science was characterized by a craftsmanlike preconception, in which a cause was deemed to "make" an effect, much as a master workman "makes" a shoe.[10] Today, the appropriate contamination of the instinct of workmanship is pecuniary enterprise.

Now, man might go on eternally altering his economic system without ever making any substantial progress, for his creative propensities would always be frustrated by some appropriate contamination. "If we could only get rid of this perennial contamination," Veblen must have said to himself, "the constructive instincts would dominate the lives of men."

10 Veblen, *The Theory of Business Enterprise*, p. 366.

He therefore examines with great care industrial employments and observes that they differ from all other methods of production that have preceded. He postulates a sort of mechanical determination and finds that the machine imposes a discipline, imparts a notion of process, inspires a realistic, matter-of-fact attitude towards life in general. The machine tends the man, as it were, and robs him of any desire for aggressive or animistic control. Thus, after scores of thousands of years, we are on the threshold of an era in which the creative instinct can learn to function without contamination among that great mass of the population which is subject to the machine discipline, engineers and factory workers, particularly. When this comes to pass, man will have laid the basis—I should like to say the moral basis—for achieving a state resembling utopia—a sort of industrial republic that Veblen nowhere describes in detail.

Utopia is not, however, the only possible destiny of mankind. The negative or contaminated propensities are copiously nourished by our social institutions. Reversion to a warlike, caste-ridden, quasi-barbaric feudal state may therefore set in before the machine has had time to perform its beneficial tasks. Since this alternative prophecy was seemingly fulfilled by the advent of fascism in Italy, nazism in Germany, and regressive military dictatorships elsewhere, his analysis has carried great conviction to some of his readers.

Thus did Veblen, with simplicity and few properties, give us, through his psychology, a master plan of past human and economic development throughout the ages, a broad panorama of the current scene, and even a good look at the future. There is much to admire in this breath-taking voyage from savagery to utopia, but also much to inspire doubt, as we shall see.

The neo-Veblenians agree with the generally accepted theories of the older man. That is, they accept Veblen's criticism of the rational, hedonistic psychology of standard theory; they seek to make their economic writings congruous with the reputable doctrines of contemporary professional psychologists, rather than with the doctrines of Bentham; they concede the importance of psychology to economics, arguing that economic behavior is only one aspect of human behavior; they believe that different men can be made to respond quite differently to the same stimulus, which is equivalent to saying that human nature has great plasticity. Up to a certain point they make man's behavior a function of his culture. In fine, their psychology is of the type of Dr. Woodworth's "middle-of-the-roaders," [11] which dominates academic thinking here and perhaps abroad.

The differences between Veblen and his followers center in the concept of the instinct of workmanship. To Veblen this was a basic instinct, buttressed by love and idle curiosity; it had, however, the fatal quality of contaminating itself, thus compelling destructive behavior. The metaphysics of this have not been acceptable to neo-Veblenians, and their writings do not depend on this proposition. A few of them do, however, use a variant form of mechanistic determinism—one that may be said to have a technocratic twist.[12] This variant doctrine holds that the potentialities of the machine will destroy the price system and that men will be forced to substitute for it an economic organization characterized by greater productivity, shorter working hours, abolition of involuntary poverty. This assumes considerable human rationality and forethought when mankind is faced with an allegedly crumbling society.

The propositions of neo-Veblenian psychological theory were well-stated by Hoxie many years ago in a few simple propositions—which, however, were not intended as a guide to institutional economic psychology. Hoxie avers:

[11] R. S. Woodworth, *Contemporary Schools of Psychology,* New York, Ronald Press, 1931, ch. vii.

[12] "Technocratic" in the sense in which the term was used popularly in 1932 to designate ideas held by Howard Scott. See Dorfman, *Thorstein Veblen and His America,* pp. 510 ff.

That man is not rational but is capable of a high degree of rationality;

That man is a product of his total social environment and inheritance;

That increased knowledge and increased association of individuals and classes will produce increased understanding, sympathy and harmony of viewpoint.

That social will is an expression of natural law.[13]

The last statement is the only obscure one. What Hoxie here means, as he himself explains, is that so-called social and economic laws are not immutable, but depend on the will of man and can therefore be changed.

These psychological assumptions and the more formal theories on which they rest provide neo-Veblenians with a basis for attacking standard economic theory, which postulates a rational man, rationally seeking his best interests. It underlies a body of knowledge known as "consumer economics" and permits all sorts of motives, such as dark sexual jealousy or light whim, sometimes to dominate the money-maker's mind. On the other hand, it admits the possibility of rational behavior (man "is capable of a high degree of rationality"). This admission permits recourse to standard theory whenever its propositions seem helpful and do not require an apology for such "rational" behavior as undeniably occurs in economic life. Both Veblen and his followers are in the strong position of being able to eat their economic man and have him too.

Hoxie's remaining propositions are appropriate to the economics of welfare and reform. Making the "social will" to be "an expression of natural law" is equivalent to scrapping all "economic laws." The neo-Veblenians are in effect saying that "economic laws" are only general, summary statements describing human behavior under present institutions. When "social will" changes these institutions, man can with his infinite capacity for adjustment, behave differently, and the "laws"—such as they are—will no longer be in effect.

13 Hoxie, *Trade Unionism in the United States*, p. 368.

This "social will" can be strengthened by education and shaped towards socially desirable ends by the constructive association of presently conflicting groups. Economic evolution is not determined in advance. It can be willed, at least within certain limits. Man can, therefore, control his economic system by making wise choices based on humane considerations.

The psychological theories of the neo-Veblenians dispose them to espouse many causes that Veblen himself would have considered futile. His system had no place for interclass understanding, conscious choices, for educational processes that would lead quarrelsome men to settle their differences by talking things out. Veblen had no objection to such things. He simply felt that men would not—at least not consistently and rigorously—support them. The only really important thing, in his view, was to get rid of that contamination of the constructive propensity. The neo-Veblenian is utterly devoid of interest in this contamination. To him social progress seems to lie in the step-by-step attenuation of conflict, not in the virtual extirpation of the aggressive propensities. This is an important difference, as we shall see.

Before going on to an appraisal of the psychology underlying institutional economics, I should complete the exposition by calling attention to a matter which arises often enough in economic writing, but receives little explicit recognition.

In recent years a psychological idea has been nibbled at that may have considerable value to institutional economists. Part of it is expressed in Pigou's optimism-pessimism theory of trade fluctuations, part is contained in the process of cumulative causation to be found in Mitchell's study of the business cycle, and Mr. Lewisohn has written about it in connection with observed behavior in manic-depressives.[14]

The notion of a cycle is often used in economic discussion.

[14] S. A. Lewisohn, "Psychology in Economics," *Political Science Quarterly*, LIII (1938), 233 ff.

We have the "vicious circle," sometimes "spiral," of inflation. The *Economist,* commenting on the Near East, once spoke of the "melancholy wheel" on which natural poverty precludes the raising of capital and lack of capital perpetuates poverty.[15] This suggests that human beings have a tendency to go to extremes, to allow themselves to get into situations from the grip of which there is no escape and in which there is no profit. When prices fall, business men dump shares and still more shares into the market—which makes prices drop even lower; when prices rise, they buy—something that makes them rise still higher. When men are poor, they seem to succeed in impoverishing themselves even farther. When banks are failing, depositors press the sound ones to pay out, thus causing more failures. The steady debilitation of the farmer, either in Rome about the time of Christ, or during the period of enclosures, or today in the American South, may flow, at least in part, from the human propensity to go from failure to even greater failure.

In brief, it seems to be clear that man tends to bring on himself greater disasters than are called for by the realities of the economic situation. Max Lerner, who may perhaps fairly be classed as a neo-Veblenian, has described the phenomenon with much understanding.

> If these are roughly the factors that brought about the stock break, there still remains the question of how it gained enough acceleration on the way down to produce for two days a frenzied panic. Empirical conditions, either in industry or in government policy, will not explain the swiftness and extent of the decline. For that we must turn to the psychological—to fear, and how it has battened on the tensions of the eight years that have elapsed since 1929.
>
> It must be remembered that what we are pleased to call the business community can become under extreme pressure a chaotic and irresponsible mob. A man who witnessed the trading on the morning of "Black Tuesday" told me that it gave him the feeling of a trampling mob in a theatre fire. There were stretches of time when blocks of "blue chip" securities, offered at almost nothing,

15 CXXXVIII (March 30, 1940), p. 558.

could not get a bid. The truth is that Wall Street men, like other organisms highly specialized for predatory pursuits, have not been able to accommodate themselves to the conditions of change. They have been battered for years by forces they cannot understand, and they are riddled with the most irrational fears. The Wall Street jungle of today is filled with Emperor Joneses. What we have regarded as the toughest and most viable of all capitalisms is at the same time as subject to panic as a frightened savage caught in a jungle at night—a jungle of his own fears, superstitions, and racial memories.[16]

The analogy of a trampling mob does not bear up, of course, for economic disasters that are slow and cumulative in effect, like a family's gradual loss of land through erosion in the course of a generation. Here failure seems to invite failure, as success breeds success; or, more technically, success tends to raise the "level of aspiration" (*Anspruchsniveau*), while failure tends to lower it.[17] In this connection Karen Horney would probably speak of "lucky circles" and vicious circles of human behavior.[18] Freud has observed that frustrated aggression tends to turn on the aggressor himself.[19] Man seems to become easily involved in downward-going spirals of increasingly desperate behavior. Mr. Lerner explains the phenomenon as one based on fear, superstition, and "racial memories," the last phrase belonging to one of the analytic schools.

Perhaps this fragment has less importance to economic theory than appears at first glance—perhaps more. It does indicate that economic phenomena are affected by a sort of accelerator principle—that is, they seem to push beyond whatever point is demanded in the situation. Prices go up or down more than they "need" to go; unemployment or business failure affect more people than is required to "correct" a

16 Max Lerner, "Notes on 'Black Tuesday,'" *The Nation* (New York, CXLV, Oct. 30, 1937), 470.

17 F. Hoppe, quoted by Brown, *Psychology and the Social Order*, p. 293.

18 K. Horney, *Neurotic Personality of Our Time*, New York, 1937, pp. 138; 226–227.

19 Freud, *New Introductory Lectures on Psycho-Analysis*, pp. 144 ff.

"disequilibrium." It seems to suggest the existence of a dialectical process in human affairs—indeed, Karen Horney tantalizingly speaks of dialectical change in the realm of individual psychology, but does not develop the point.[20] Perhaps there is here a suggestion as to how government should intervene to promote greater welfare. Perhaps certain crises would have only limited repercussions if the public authority decreed the prompt freezing of prices or the immediate, but temporary, closing of markets and banks, or an instant moratorium or exchange control, or the prompt granting of loans on generous terms to special groups. The last dozen years have seen most of these types of intervention in the United States, and they have no doubt contributed to the general welfare, but they may have failed to exert full effect, because their relation to human behavior was not clearly seen. Perhaps a better understanding of the underlying psychology will bring about better methods of control, if they are desired.

Something of importance may eventually disengage itself from a study of what may be named circular behavior. The importance of this topic seems to arise from the fact that such behavior is motivated neither by aggression alone nor by economic self-interest nor by the constructive propensities. In other words, it explains certain economic phenomena by a human trait which neither standard theorists nor Veblen nor neo-Veblenians have tried hard to understand. It seems to lie at the basis of Mitchell's "description" of the business cycle, a description that "is not merely empirical—it must accord with reason." [21] I think it throws light on the frequency of a public policy of drift—that is, the tendency of governments to let economic dislocations continue to the point of crisis—at which point intervention becomes more restrictive than it would have been had prompt action been taken earlier.

20 K. Horney, *op. cit., passim.*

21 Clark, "Wesley C. Mitchell's Contribution to the Theory of Business Cycles," in *Preface to Social Economics,* pp. 402 ff.

Veblen recognized the existence of this phenomenon of "unnecessarily" wide swings. If I understand him aright, he says that powerful forces, or interests, in the background desire disturbances of great amplitude, because change is favorable to the making of money, and the greater the disturbance, the larger the amount of money made.[22] I am skeptical of this analysis, partly because it seems to vest too much power in too few hands, but also because in so thinking Veblen showed concern only for amplitude—straight up-and-down motion, as it were. Realizing how dangerous are any analogies to physics, I venture to affirm that the process is more nearly spiral than linear. In other words, the swing is not merely up-and-down, over the same territory, again and again. A severe depression, like a great war, carries us into a new area, where those who might have benefited from uncomplicated motions, are ruined by the complexity of the forces loosed.

We begin our evaluation of institutional psychology by striking at Veblen's most vulnerable point: his theory of social change, brought about by man's association with machinery. There is nothing to support the hypothesis that the machine is competent to eradicate aggressive (or animistic) tendencies. Veblen's solution seems to be to apply the old educational theory of formal discipline, which has long been discredited. As early as 1890 William James's inquiries into the theory raised doubts; but Veblen was, apparently, so blinded by his need to find a utopian solution to his problem that he overlooked the existing studies.[23] One might, in passing, ask whether the machine-age worker during factory hours is really under the influence of process rather than of mere cause-and-effect relationships. Is it not a matter of common knowledge that the microscopic division of labor of the ma-

22 Veblen, *The Instinct of Workmanship,* pp. 353 ff.

23 For an interesting collection of educational and psychological opinions on this question see C. E. Skinner, ed., *Readings in Educational Psychology,* New York, 1937, ch. xvi.

chine industry is precisely what prevents the worker from being much exposed to notions of process on the job? [24]

The question at issue, stated in appropriate psychological terms, seems to be whether contact with the machine process deepens man's ability to make contact with reality, to eschew animism, ideological bias, unfounded hopes, self-directed or unsublimated aggression, unconstructive satisfactions. Psychoanalysts face this problem daily, and one of their chief tasks is to help their patients maintain contact with the real external world and turn bootless aggression into constructive channels. Despite their use in this process of occupational therapy and their insistence on the role of work and even muscular work in fruitful living, none has, as far as I know, recommended the boring mill, the drill press, or the automatic screw machine.

Remaining strictly inside the Veblenian framework, with nothing else altered, one important thing is lost if we accept the argument that Veblen's way to utopia is a dead-end street —that is, hope. If we strike out mechanical determinism as a saving force, we are left no prospect other than that of regression to a semi-barbarous state, not unlike the feudal state, or perhaps like Nazi Germany. But absence of hope is not proof of error. To be sure, Veblen, in his later writings, saw Russia as an independent source of hope, probably through the process of cultural diffusion, a process in itself not inconsistent with his psychological theory or other acceptable theories. This was all very well for Veblen two decades ago. The question for us to answer is whether the Russians have anything to diffuse that mitigates or sublimates the aggressive

[24] In a note on page 343 of the *Instinct of Workmanship* Veblen indicates that perhaps the "Syndicalists" are the first to show the effects of exposure to the machine process. If by "Syndicalists" he means the Industrial Workers of the World, the example is badly chosen. Members of the I.W.W. were, for the most part, miners, migratory workers, lumberjacks, and agricultural workers—occupations that were not highly mechanized when Veblen wrote. Indeed, the introduction of machinery into these occupations seems to have contributed to the extinction of the organization. See my *Decline of the I.W.W.*, New York, Columbia University Press, 1932, pp. 180 ff.

propensities.[25] Certainly there has been no clear proof that predation and coercion are dead in the Soviet Union, though some slight evidence may seem to point towards an inchoate movement in that direction. We must be sure, in making an appraisal, that absence of our kind of coercion is not mistaken for a complete absence of coercion in the acquisition of economic goods. We must ask what methods are applied to remove the harmfully aggressive propensities and where? In the schools? The home? The youth organizations? Has the USSR a clearly stated psychological theory to back up its methods, if there are methods?

Mitchell, who follows Veblen to the point of expecting no magical changes in the psyche and lacks the eagerness of many neo-Veblenians, finds a source of hope in the possibilities of psychological discovery. For many this will appear to be a slender cord on which to suspend hope, but at least it is better than to be left with nothing at all, which is where we found ourselves two paragraphs ago.

The theory of mechanical determinism represents the high-water mark of Veblen's psychological error. What is left of his theory can be dealt with more gently. It conforms, as we have seen, to a basic Freudian doctrine, which, if not generally and explicitly accepted by academic psychologists, has exerted a strong influence in the psychological theory of the last quarter century. Whether right or wrong, the psychology adopted accords with the economic theory developed. Never before, indeed, have economics and psychology walked together so compatibly in happy marriage. The basic principles discussed in the last chapter are all in harmony with Veblen's doctrines concerning human behavior. Nevertheless, there is room for minor doubts, at least.

One weakness of his coercion theory, for example, is that Veblen is not very clear about the incidence of the destructive

[25] The military successes of the Russians cannot, alone, be adduced as proof of the error of Veblen's Russian assumptions. Socially desirable aggression may coexist in a personality activated by the constructive propensities.

tendencies. The reader carries away the belief that Aryans are congenitally more aggressive than non-Aryans; that the Japanese are highly aggressive because, though industrial, they are still near feudalism—something that makes the Germans highly aggressive even among Aryans. Everywhere engineers and the working class manifest fewer destructive propensities than businessmen, lawyers, educators, or the clergy. Yet he has castigated the narrow pecuniary interest, hence recognized the aggression potential, of trade unionism. In Freudian theory, though there are individual differences, there is no major emphasis on class-determined aggression.

If the Freudian and post-Freudian views were rigorously applied to Veblen's economic doctrine, some amendments would probably have to be made to Veblenian theory, but not many, I venture to think. This applies to the economic doctrines *in sensu strictu;* his theory of social change would require radical revision. His basic theories concerning the division of employments into pecuniary and industrial categories would not require alteration—on the contrary, they would be rooted in even deeper soil, for Freudians have some original contributions of their own to make here. Price would still be what the traffic will bear; collusion and chicanery would still pervade the process of exchange—or, rather, there would be no exchange, but rather a process of foisting-upon-and-palming off instead. There would be disorganization, business cycles, chronic unemployment, and the disemboweling of natural wealth. International warfare, though not the direct result of economic causes, would be a phenomenon congruous with the other phenomena of economic life.

The similarity of goals between Freud and Veblen is most striking. Veblen's hope is to organize all of life, particularly economic life, around the constructive rather than the destructive propensities. Freud's noneconomic and allegedly-nonsocial theories of individual behavior move him to organize the life of his patient around the constructive propensities and the sublimated aggressions. If the psychologist has set his goal without benefit of moral speculations, is it not possible that economics, through psychology, may set economic goals that have roots, not in ethical speculation, but in science? It is also interesting to note that what hope for the future is held out by Mitchell moves in the same direction as does Freud's, namely, towards the development of the intelligence and the strengthening of the constructive propensities. "The voice of the intellect is feeble, but it is persistent."

Some Communist readers may feel that the last few pages have been disturbingly tendentious, and others that a fraudulent maneuver has been executed by assimilating Veblenism to Freudianism. Such readers will, perhaps, condemn the insidious process by which I have managed to find similarities between that peerless American rebel Thorstein Veblen and the decadent, bourgeois apologist and counterrevolutionary Sigmund Freud. The Russians have given special treatment to Freud as Julian Huxley, after returning from the celebration of the 220th anniversary of the Russian Academy of Sciences in 1945, observes:

> The only field of natural science where Marxist theory seems to have an effect is that of psychology. True to the materialist principles of Marxism, Russian investigators appear to confine themselves almost entirely to the behavioristic and physiological approach, leaving out the mental aspects. Thus Freudian psychoanalysis, as well as introspective psychology of the classical kind, seem to be taboo—or at any rate are not studied.[26]

This special treatment is very difficult to understand; one wonders whether it is based on faithful study of Freud's works, or whether it is based on unexplored prejudice.

The psychological theories of neo-Veblenians raise two questions in my mind. One refers to rational behavior, the other to the attenuation of aggression. The younger institutionalists have made no revision of Hoxie's statement that

[26] Julian Huxley, "A Scientist Goes to Russia," *New Republic,* CXIII (July 30, 1945), 126.

"man is not rational but is capable of a high degree of rationality." This double-acting statement is most confusing. It is meaningless unless one makes an honest attempt to define when and under what circumstances men act rationally in economic affairs and when irrationally—since both forms of behavior are provided for.

I submit that man acts most rationally to attain immediate and often unsubstantial goals and least rationally to obtain distant and constructive goals. To convert this into useful economic language we may say that men act less rationally in situations that contribute to economic organization and most rationally in situations that lead to economic disorganization. For exmple, the person who buys in the black market may behave rationally in the simple mechanics of purchase, but his contribution towards possible inflation and breakdown of economic control is irrational.

Now, the fundamental hypothesis of standard theory is that immediate, short-range, selfish, unenlightened economic actions are, through the magic of the competitive process, transmogrified into long-range organizing forces. Mankind would indeed be blest if this were true. And it would be a most defensible hypothesis if one small premise of standard theory were valid, namely, that competition is vigorous, legal, and dominated by a spirit of fair play. But competition is either cut-throat or lethargic; it is sometimes without the law and often barely within it, and it has great ethical flexibility. Thus, competition becomes coercion and has but a small organizing function.

What lies behind competition lies also behind all nonautomatic forms of organization. When government attempts to organize economic effort, or when business, labor, and public representatives, through codes or agreements, attempt to unravel the tangled skein of economic life, all parties subject to regulation attempt to infract the rules—to perform acts that are rational enough on the short-term view, but that destroy the intended organization of economic activity. By seeking to get benefits through disorganizing behavior, human beings deprive themselves of the enhanced productivity that only economic organization can bring. This, I think, defines the chief area of economic irrationality.

Some such distinction underlies rational and irrational behavior in individual psychology. All behavior is rational, Freud has said, if the goal is understood. Jeremy Bentham worked out similar ideas with considerable elaboration, and his scale of the value of pleasures according to duration, intensity, fecundity, purity, and other qualities has applicability to the instant discussion. Surely among the goals of sane living are, on the one hand, to increase the capacity to discover fructifying satisfactions and, when needful, to await greater though deferred satisfactions; on the other hand, to diminish a taste for sterile or self-destroying pleasures, many of which require no postponement. It is doubtful whether modern psychologists would hold—as institutionalists might seem to suggest [27]—that one need be skilled in hedonistic calculation to follow such a way of life. What is important is that there be basic clarity in the personality concerning a few major goals and the absence of great conflict between conscious and unconscious desires. If the personality be well launched, we need not worry about its ability, on the whole, to make rational decisions—though there will be occasional lapses from rationality (the danger of total destruction of personality through catastrophe is always a possibility, of course). The process of acting rationally is like the process of maintaining good physical health. Given a good body, good nourishment, a few facts about health, the standard immunizations, men can go through life with very little illness and without engaging constantly in lightning calculations of how to escape disease. Rational behavior is not much different.

I hope I have not made the rational way of life sound too

[27] See Mitchell, "Benthams' Felicific Calculus," in *The Backward Art of Spending Money and Other Essays*, pp. 177–203.

easy. I meant only to argue that living rationally does not require constant hedonistic calculation, as suggested by most institutional theorists. Human rationality has been made to sound impossible by institutionalists, because they have assumed that one could behave rationally only under the psychic mechanisms conceived in the early nineteenth century and the task imposed by these mechanisms was indeed incapable of fulfillment. I am arguing that rational behavior in respect of long-term goals is possible, but difficult, especially difficult in matters contributing towards economic organization, and that the mechanism does not require felicific calculation, but an absence of too-great conflict between conscious and unconscious goals.

This discussion of rationality may best close on a semantic note. The word "rational" is a dubious one. It has for so many centuries been associated with a false concept of the mind that we may properly discard it as having no useful meaning. Until new concepts arise to define economic behavior, we shall not advance far if we speak of it as being either rational, irrational, or sometimes the one and sometimes the other.

The second point I should like to make concerns the desire of the neo-Veblenians, in their practical program, to attenuate human conflict in various ways. Can conflict be, in fact, attenuated, or can only violence be attenuated? In other words, can genuine progress be made in mitigating economic coercion simply by attenuating its violence? Let us for the moment accept the story that cavemen took economic goods away from each other by appropriately vigorous use of a gnarled club, while modern men achieve the same end by monetary policies, or misleading statements, or by influencing legislation. Has a psychological change been wrought? If so, are there substantial economic repercussions? If there have been economic gains, have they been overrated by most of us? I shall drop the subject here to take it up again, in a slightly altered setting, in the next chapter.

The theories of human behavior relied upon by Hoxie and the other neo-Veblenians would probably be accepted by a larger group of psychologists than would accept Veblen's. The younger men have been more cautious and have not strayed far from what is generally approved. It is, therefore, not easy to make any further evaluation of their psychology—at least, not from the viewpoint of psychology.

From the viewpoint of economics something can, in fairness I think, be said. There is probably no science that has been developed exclusively by its practitioners. Pasteur was neither a biologist nor a physician, yet his great discoveries were contributions to biology and to medicine. Currently, astronomers and physicists contribute to each others' sciences. Perhaps the time has come when we can expect the economist to make occasional contributions to psychology. The special needs of his science require him to check against theories of human behavior from time to time. If the psychologists have nothing useful to offer in the solution of a problem, the economist should feel free to invent his psychology as he needs it—remembering always, of course, that the usual limits placed on free invention do not permit him to devise extravagant explanations. All knowledge must hold together.

Nearly half a century has passed since Veblen's basic ideas have been available in print. Two generations of economic scholars have matured, many of whom have accepted his influence, used his phrases, and worked with some of his ideas. From none of them has come a single valuable psychological insight. Indeed, it can be argued that the opposite is true, that they have by neglect buried Veblen's most interesting psychological insights.

The fact is that neo-Veblenians do not require much psychological wisdom, because they do not handle very difficult theoretical problems. Nothing has encouraged them to enrich what theory they have. Much of their written work is monographic and atomistic; much of their practical work is that of neo-cameralism. They are concerned with the standard reforms of social democracy or with variations of the doctrines of Keynes and Hansen. In this work, so important and so useful today, they may need to know some of the practical psychology of the politician or the statesman, but empiric wisdom of this sort is not a sufficient basis for theoretical work.

The neo-Veblenians are properly accused of not having developed institutional economic theory. I think the reason is that they have quite understandably mistrusted Veblenian psychology; on the other hand, they have not poured out sweat or tears to develop a more fruitful concept of the human soul. I do not think they should be too sharply censured on this account. Many of them were about thirty years old when Veblen died, in 1929, and had only begun to think their own thoughts. Since then the world has been in a state of grave and permanent emergency. Economists have, in the past fifteen years, been asked to put their shoulders to the wheel, to extemporize, improvise, and count. They have met day-to-day problems with great success; they fed the hungry in 1932 and sustained a withering volume of production; they have given the hope of security to the common man; they have planned for a fantastic production flow in the past few years of war; they have told their airmen where to strike the enemy's sources of war material; they are planning the reconstruction of a devastated world. There has been no time to steep the mind in psychological theory; many of them have been too tired after the day's highly responsible work to go in for rumination. In the meantime, they have tended to believe, but without careful inspection, that the evolution of pure theory is as vain as was the elaboration of medieval scholasticism. Perhaps they are wrong.

III METHODOLOGY

THE FIRST difference generally noted between the methodology of standard economic theory and that of institutional theory is that the former is deductive while the latter is inductive. Although this observation is superficial, it has a rough elementary usefulness. The next most generally accepted proposition about institutional methodology is that it relies on statistics, the "genetic approach," and description. This, too, is a useful statement, but for beginners only.

A study of Veblen's methodology may be divided into two parts: first, his critique of the method of his contemporaries and their predecessors in standard theory; second, his own positive contributions to methodology. The latter, like his psychology, can be subdivided farther into his conscious, expressed, explicit method and his unconscious methodological habits.

We shall not dwell on his criticisms of standard theory, since they are generally known. They are briefly stated as follows: standard theory is based on certain erroneous assumptions, such as the existence of natural rights, natural order, normal order, a pleasure-pain calculator in the psyche; it relies on conjectural history to justify and explain contemporary institutions; it deals with normal cases, and departures from the assumed norm are dismissed as unimportant—a procedure that results in a system of economic taxonomy. Standard theory has a strong ideological [1] bias, in that it is impregnated with the preconceptions of a predacious mode of living; it confuses the creation of property rights with the creation of goods and services. In sum, it uses the

[1] See Mannheim, Karl. *Ideology and Utopia,* New York, Harcourt Brace, 1936.

animistic method, sufficiently disguised, however, in the raiment of science to pass uncritical inspection. As for the historical and Marxian methods, the former, though of good augury, has disappointed expectations; the latter, neo-Hegelian and pre-Darwinian, lends itself to error.

Veblen's positive, explicit methodological principles also need not delay us long. They have become well known. He believed himself to be a Darwinian, hence one who applied the concepts of "evolutionary science" to economics. He demanded the "opaque fact" and the uprooting of animism in economic thought. He was relatively lacking in ideological bias. His emphasis was on function rather than structure; he preferred the living whole to the dismembered parts. Probably he would have approved—though perhaps without enthusiasm—what is contained in current books on the techniques of research: good sampling, use of controls when possible, and so forth. His lack of the usual human vanities enabled him to find new meanings in ordinary phenomena.

The most interesting part of his methodology is the part least regarded. He is, for example, a determinist of great consistency; he uses the hypothetico-deductive method; [2] he was at least as much addicted to the notion of dialectical change as to that of evolutionary development. Throughout, he uses methodological concepts similar to those of recent contemporary Gestalt sociologists. Let us take up these points in turn, beginning with determinism.

Veblen's determinism, though forming a unified scheme, can be broken up into at least three units for convenient examination. The first is that of the determining role of the cultural pattern or type of social organization. Nothing, for example, can be done in a society dominated by the spirit of business enterprise that is not congruous with that spirit. What is taught in the schools, preached in the churches,

[2] This will be described below. I first noted this adjective in Brown, *Psychology and the Social Order.*

sought for in the laboratories—all are inevitable manifestations of a central theme. In this he is not original by any means, reminding us of Sombart, Marx, and the economic historians. He does seem to recognize an independent free-floating realm of ideas, the domain of the instinct of idle curiosity. Veblen's own ideas might be proof of the existence of such a free port; he himself seemed to believe this. Certain accidental impacts could affect any cultural pattern. Cultural diffusion would be one kind of accident; warfare and invention would be other types. On the whole, one gathers from Veblen the impression that, though any stage or form of social organization permits change or variation and tolerates vestiges of past cultural patterns (culture lags), the dominating theme remains the same. The organizing or activating principle is, in a sense, static. The social costs of changing from one form of organization to another are high and may inspire recourse to violence. When a cultural pattern is broken, the word "broken" has no figurative meaning, but really involves dislocation, sundering, disorder, shattering.

A second aspect of Veblenian determinism we have already discussed at length, namely, occupational determinism—that is, the effect of pecuniary or industrial pursuits on their practitioners. The third type is what might be named self-generating change. The essence of this concept is that, though a culture remains congruous within itself and rejects any attempt at major alterations, certain processes nevertheless do go on within that culture to undermine it and to bring about change. Incidentally, Mitchell uses the concept of self-generating change on a smaller scale in his work on the business cycle.

Perhaps it will assist comprehension if one associates this process with the unseen burrowing of termites or with the hidden-ball trick of baseball, since it resembles both. A complete understanding of this aspect of Veblen's determinism provides the answer to this question: can a certain type of social organization change radically if there are no accidents, such as cultural diffusion, or invention, or other special circumstance (for example, the Black Death)? The answer—for those who follow Veblen—is "yes."

The reason I have spoken of termites and the hidden-ball trick is that the force—the very potent force—that is competent to break up a cultural pattern is invisible, hidden, unnoticed by most persons. What savage, to use a Veblenian example, living under primitive communism, thoughtlessly and happily exercising his instinct of workmanship several score millennia ago, could have realized that the very process of making valuable objects would inspire the cupidity of others, subject him to attack, to the introduction of the concept of private property, therefore to the abolition of primitive communism, and, finally, to the atrophy of his instinct of workmanship under slavery? In other words, the productive, unwarlike society, precisely because it was productive and unwarlike, had within it the seeds of its own destruction. Whether some savage Veblen of those days saw the handwriting on the wall and warned his fellows, we do not know. Had there been one, his contemporaries would probably have labeled him an institutionalist, laughed at his ironic humor, and noted that his criticism was not constructive.

As has already been said, a society like ours, in which the spirit of business enterprise finds its peak of fulfillment in machinofacture, will be changed because that process inspires the mass to disregard the institutional bases on which business enterprise rests.

Presumably the basic changes between the period of primitive communism and the present have not been great, though there has been considerable pulling and hauling during the period of recorded history. When all is said and done, the changes do not amount to much. Women of this era and of western culture wear high heels instead of disks in the lobes of their ears; the underlying population, Veblen would say, is fooled by the cinema and the newspaper instead of by the king and the priest; the conscientious withholding of efficiency in industrial processes by trade union leader and financier is not unlike the feudal baron's rude insistence on tribute at the bridge or ford. Dark, sinister, and predatory forces in the background behave today as they did a thousand, three thousand, or five thousand years ago. We recognize a Tweed in the plays of Aristophanes; the vulgarities of Petronius's Trimalchio are no different from those of America's Gilded Age.

For the current situation, however, Veblen believes that a subtler force is at work and that alterations, this time, may amount to a very great deal. He establishes his redetermining agents with the skill of a dramatist who in an early scene casually shows us the fatal revolver to be used in a later scene. Veblen early establishes both the constructive and the animistic propensities of man, either of which eventually may destroy the spirit of business enterprise. From the viewpoint of procedure, one is forced to admire Veblen's workmanship, whatever the merits of his argument.

Veblen's determinism thus turns out to be a sort of closed system in which man, his institutions, and the pattern they create, move, and change only within circumscribed areas—at least, for the calculable future. Though he may be willing to accept the psychological plasticity of James or even of the behaviorists, the Western, civilized world, its traditions being what they are, must accept either of certain forseeable and ineluctable outcomes, completely determined by what is and by what has gone before. "Nothing can deflect the sweep of business enterprise, unless it be an outgrowth of this enterprise itself or of the industrial means by which business enterprise works." [3] Certain accidents outside his universe may, of course, upset this, such as a new ice age or the collision of planets; accidents of another sort may determine whether the future state will be the neo-feudal state or the utopian industrial republic. But no accident within his universe can forestall its inevitables.

A second notable characteristic of Veblen's method is originality and concern for the broad generalization. There is no

[3] *Theory of Business Enterprise,* pp. 378–379.

question but that Veblen gave us new insights into economic processes and that his skillful blending of economics with psychology surpasses anything of the sort previously done in economics. Whether we agree or disagree with him, any fair estimate of his work must concede that he drew on springs of inspiration that are inaccessible to most of us. No doubt some of his inspiration was the result of an extraordinary mental endowment, perhaps hereditary. But some of his inspiration was also the result of one element of his methodology—an element that Stuart Chase has described as the "hunch" method and elsewhere has been more elegantly described as the "hypothetico-deductive" method.[4] It is pointed out that Veblen is inconsistent—that the man who insistently yells for the opaque fact himself pulls theories out of his hat, his sleeve or out of thin air—as brazenly as ever did the deductive, taxonomic, pre-Darwinian, and yet otherwise benighted standard theorist.

The accusation contains truth. Whether it is as damning as it sounds will receive consideration in a later section. At this point we cite only a few extenuating circumstances. Veblen came late to economic writing and only after constructing a world pattern for himself out of elements drawn from a wide variety of experiences. The latter included his early rural surroundings, the overseas cultural heritage of his family, the formal study of philosophy and experience of the large urban centers. Without the preconceptions of the professional economist he read some of the most important American documents on the actual functioning of the economic system—the 19 volumes of the *Report* of the Industrial Commission. His mind was at least as well stocked as that of any contemporary scholar, and perhaps he was more alert than others to turn daily observation to account—from the slogans used by small-town civic associations to the perennial monstrosity of women's hats. All this and a developed sense of humor and insight into the unconscious motivations of mankind impelled him to seek truth as the novelist or the poet seeks it.

4 See Brown, *Psychology and the Social Order.*

The willingness, or the courage, possessed by Veblen to put forth his hypotheses is quite as striking as his intelligence and is at one with the courage he demonstrated in holding fast to the principle of determinism. Perhaps courage is part of any methodology and an important ingredient of inspiration.

A third facet of Veblen's methodology is his use of something like the Hegelian dialectic. I think it is important to return again—at the risk of trying the reader's patience—to his theory that the machine's effect on man, if sufficiently prolonged, will result in the strengthening of the constructive propensities and will make possible the coming into existence of an industrial republic. And I cite again the Veblenian argument that, though our civilization may introduce the social insurances, may mitigate the evils of unemployment by various means, and may accept in many areas the democratic processes of compromise and collective bargaining—in spite of all this apparent "progress," we may suddenly find ourselves plunged, according to Veblen, regressively into a civilization of violence and status. This is not exactly genetic process; it is dialectical change. Where is our "evolutionary" scientist now, and where the Veblen who rebuked Marx for his Hegelian "point of departure"?

A fourth characteristic of Veblen's method, though unmistakable, is difficult to name. The currently-fashionable word "global" will perhaps serve as well as any other to express part of the intended idea. His view is not parochial, and he moves easily up and down the centuries. But he is the master of things other than mere time and space. He attempts—though not always with success—to square his economics with the knowledge he has of the other sciences. His economic principles are placed against a background not only of institutions but also of relevant bodies of knowledge, such as biology, psychology, anthropology, ethnology, and history. I think he set great store by this characteristic of his work and that it was an important ingredient of what he named—or misnamed—the "evolutionary" approach.

Another part of the intended idea is his relative lack of egocentrism; unlike Anatole France's dog, he did not believe himself to be the center of the universe—and in Veblen's case the absence of egocentrism applied to time as well as to space. He understood, for example, that when (if) savages exchanged two beavers for one deer, the considerations would probably not be the same as those obtaining among moderns engaging in barter or sale-and-purchase. On the other hand, there was something egocentric in his belief that the present was either the threshold of the industrial republic or the turning point in a regressive process. In this he did not equal the as-yet unsurpassed Jovian attitudes of Fourier, who interposed two stages between the present and his final utopian goal.

Despite occasional backsliding, he avoided a kind of pluralism or atomism that distinguishes inquiry in the sciences when they are still young. To the earliest biologists, astronomers, or chemists anthropomorphism accompanies pluralism and atomism. Thus, Buffon's lion "a la figure imposante, le regard assuré, la démarche fière, la voix terrible." The modern zoologist tries to see lions against their proper background of the animal world, not the world of human beings; as the creatures they are, not as beasts having human qualities, be they bourgeois or seigniorial. Gold is no longer the king of metals, but an element seen against the background of Mendeleef's tabular chart; the stars are no longer a motley crew of transmogrified demi-gods and mortals, but an integrated system of masses held together in dynamic equilibrium. Veblen felt that a distinguishing feature of modern science was to conceive of everything as part of a larger setting, and his work is marked by this conception; this he sometimes seems to confuse with the idea of evolution.

This global or universal quality was a form of absolutism. Veblen would probably have denied that one form of economic theory was more appropriate to London's city men than to the nomads of the Near East before Christ or to American Indians before Columbus. His great generalizations, if they did not cover all cases, applied to several cultures and to more centuries than one. If I am right in this, I contradict those who believe that Veblen conceives of one kind of economic theory as being appropriate under one set of institutions, while another type is appropriate to another set. People who hold this view sometimes speak of economic relativity, or the relativity of economic doctrines. This seems a misuse of the word "relativity" for the revolution in epistemology suggested by Einstein gives impetus to the quest for ever more inclusive generalizations. The errors engendered by a relative view can only stimulate the search for a more nearly general statement.

One final aspect of globality must be pointed out. Veblen's methodological compulsion to place a subject in its broader setting leads him into the other sciences to such a degree that economics seems at times to be forgotten. He then seemingly becomes a social philosopher or, at the very least, a sociologist. This invites the criticism that Veblen expanded the scope of economics beyond the point to which it should go. Examination of the validity of this criticism will come later; only its existence is noted here.

We now leave Veblen to see what the neo-Veblenians have been doing. They agree with Veblen that the "deductive" method of standard theory is, if not sterile, then at least unfruitful at this stage of the development of economic theory. They are eager to find the "opaque fact" and to avoid the so-called "abstract" method. Addicted to statistics, they do not use the methods of mathematical economists. On the contrary, the mathematicians are suspect in the institutionalists' world. Neo-Veblenians formulate good questionnaires, report interviews with safeguards against failure of memory or simple bias, appraise accurately the value of newspapers, trade-union journals, or minutes of meetings as sources. Their study of mathematics, statistics, and logic has warned them against the pitfalls of interpolation, extrapolation, faulty sampling, concluding too much from coefficients of correlation, or omitting consideration of probable error. They do a tidy job, in brief. All of this is in paradoxical agreement with Veblen, since it conforms to his doctrines, though not so obviously to his practice. Like him, they are not much handicapped by ideological bias. Unlike him, they avoid the hypothetico-deductive method and his unconsciously neo-Hegelian procedures.

Neo-Veblenians have not concerned themselves much about the larger issues of methodology, though a few scattered things may be found here and there. In the appendix to his book on trade-unionism Hoxie makes a few notes—apparently they are not intended to be more than that—on method. He suggests to the student: firstly, that the latter describe a phenomenon only after direct, careful observation; secondly, that he try to explain how it came into being or how it evolved. Here he cautions against a random historical excursion and insists on a search for the determining factors. These two steps are fairly standard ones in the writings of institutionalists. Perhaps a third could be added: How will this phenomenon appear in the future? This three-step scheme was used by Veblen, and most institutionalists would willingly undertake many of their investigations with these three questions as their guides: What is this like? How did it come to be as it is? What will it be like tomorrow? Perhaps it is just barely worth noting that Mr. and Mrs. Charles Beard, who admire Veblen, do not use this three-step procedure, though F. J. Turner [5] does.

Wesley Mitchell has written a few stray words on methodology, particularly in relation to statistics. His main point seems to be that "in preparing for their work, the quantitative theorists usually find it necessary to formulate problems in a way different from that adopted by qualitative theorists." In this context, at least, it is probably fair to assume that quantitative includes "institutional," while "qualitative" includes

[5] F. J. Turner, *The Frontier in American History*, New York, Holt, 1920.

"standard." Elsewhere he congratulates contemporary economists on their avoidance of such methodological quarrels as took place in the quarter century that closed in 1904. He intimates that "increasing concern with factual observations" and the subsidence of debate over "broad issues" are evidences of sound health in current economic thought.[6] From my contact with him when a student I should guess, however, that his fundamental dislike is not for methodology, but for the sterile quarrels of half a century ago; his actual unconcern with methodology is merely a result of vigorous interests elsewhere.

Neo-Veblenians are well aware of the criticisms made by Homan [7] and others that they have not developed a rounded theory of economic life, that their work is monographic and dedicated to special problems. They do not seem to be much bothered by this criticism, for various reasons. They apparently feel that any rounded theory must be based on an accumulation of facts or factual studies so broad that more time is needed to build up the groundwork; it is premature to theorize. Also, they probably believe that science is too vast to be confined by a few hypotheses; there may be useful general statements, but their integration is, even eventually, impossible. Institutionalists probably do not realize how often they fall back on the "laws" of standard economics; in other words, they dodge creating theories of their own by using, more liberally than they realize, the theories of standard economics. Finally, they are persuaded both by their pragmatism and by their genuinely humanitarian bent that as much solid work is being accomplished without theory as could ever be accomplished with theory. Their work is thus monographic and distinguished by atomism. It is on the level of artisanship, most excellent artisanship, which rarely even aspires to the level of creation. The high-water mark of their atomistic work has at times been characterized by words such as: "ana-

6 *The Backward Art of Spending Money*, pp. 404–405.
7 *Encyclopedia of the Social Sciences*, article on "Economics"; subsection on "Institutional Economics."

lytic," "synthetic," "descriptive, but informed by theory," and so forth. What this seems to mean is that the work tends towards some important general statement, but towards one ranking under a "law" or "principle" in the hierarchy of science. Certainly a host of interesting and valuable generalizations have come out of institutionalist writings: that intellectuals have little place in the labor movements; that governmental intervention is more easily tolerated in war than in peace; that agricultural prices are less "sticky" than industrial prices—to give only a few examples. The problem of building up higher generalizations from those lower in degree is a fascinating one, first called to my attention by Thomas Alexander, of Teachers College, Columbia University; but it is one into which we cannot go except to say that neo-Veblenians have done nothing much about it.

The neo-Veblenians do not accept the older man's strict determinism. Admitting much of the force of Veblen's argument, they would deny its completeness. There can be no closed system, they would say, where the human mind is. The cortex responds to environmental stimuli, but in turn demonstrably shapes the environment. In a process of action and interaction of this sort, it is idle to speak of a few limited determinants. The younger men, electic, where Veblen was philosophical and fastidiously logical, would place faith in such things as public education, a free press, and an expanding democracy—and, in characteristically pragmatic fashion, place faith in faith itself.

There is an important difference between the determinism of Veblen and that of the neo-Veblenians; it can be illustrated by a crude example and by putting words into the mouths of Veblen and Hoxie that were never spoken. Veblen would say: "A passenger having accidentally fallen out of an aeroplane in flight will strike the ground and be killed. He can wave his arms, pray, protest, or even deny that he is falling—nothing will avail. Our passenger's fate is determined the moment he inadvertently quits the plane." Hoxie would say: 'Though the law of gravity is inflexible, it can be circumvented by human intelligence and the human will. A passenger, forced to abandon his plane in flight, may be killed, of course, as Veblen says. Another, by forethought, may have strapped a parachute to his back, and will survive. It is true that each must accept the determinants of his situation; on the other hand each has at least some freedom to determine his situation."

The reader will see that different things are being discussed and that both disputants are right. The real disagreement is whether we are talking about a man already hurtling between heaven and earth without a parachute, or one still free to get a chute and strap it on. In other words, is our social system completely launched and unable to alter its destination, or are we still in a position to make choices?

Mitchell is less committed to the typically neo-Veblenian view. In some areas, at least, and at times he leaves the impression of being a fairly strict determinist. Granted that economic activities operate in the field of the coercive pecuniary system, he argues, there must be business cycles. Moreover, depression inevitably begets recovery and boom, and vice versa. Although he seems to feel that men, by conscious intervention, by high purpose and knowledge, can save themselves from some of the ills they call down on their own heads, he also seems to lack much fervor in this faith. Perhaps he feels only that his faith will not be realized until we know more than we now do about the human mind in general and about the behavior of man as economic agent in particular.

Evaluation of institutional methodology presents real problems to one who is not completely a philosopher, and it is with diffidence that I now formally attempt to appraise the methods by which Veblen and neo-Veblenians have attempted to ferret out useful facts and generalizations.

Let us begin with some of the easier jobs. On the whole, little fault is to be found with Veblen's negative contributions, namely, his unflattering estimate of the methodology of standard theory. Veblen was quite correct in saying that the similarity between the method of standard theory and physics or astronomy simply does not exist and that only a studied self-deception aided by the specious use of words such as "law," "statics," "dynamics," and "equilibrium" could long maintain the illusion of similarity. Perhaps his criticisms were too harsh; perhaps he did not give sufficient weight to the important economic discoveries made with bad tools; perhaps he placed too much emphasis on his own "evolutionary" method. Indeed, the "evolutionary" attitude, on his own analysis, turns out to be a "spiritual attitude" [8] rather than something he can define clearly. To modern scientists drafts from the *Origin of Species* are no longer heady; but things were different fifty years ago.

If Veblen were writing today, one feels that he would not be riding the Rozinante of evolution, but rather the thriftier steed of organismic theory. Some of his more obscure methodological phrases seem to fit the Gestalt theoretical (or organismic) approach—such expressions as "cumulative causation," "process," "genetic study," "economic life process," "the more comprehensive schemes of sequence and relation."

I do not describe organismic theory at any length, partly because such a task is beyond the scope of this book, but principally because the matter has been very adequately presented in English and has even become available in textbook form. I refer to the work of B. F. Brown and his teachers Cassirer and Lewin. By borrowing liberally from Mr. Brown I can, however, suggest some of the leading ideas.[9] The postulate is first made that energy exists in organized systems and that man is one of these. The second postulate is that the whole is greater than the parts and that therefore there is no local determination. The existing structure of the field determines the local event, not the local event the structure of the field;

[8] Veblen, *The Place of Science in Modern Civilization,* p. 60.
[9] Brown, *Psychology and the Social Order,* pp. 28 ff.

causation is from the whole to parts. Physics, biology, psychology, and the social sciences are not so far apart as is often supposed, since under this view all of them are amenable to the propositions of the logic of dynamics.

The concepts of organismic theory are primarily functional rather than substantial, and scientific analysis is, therefore, primarily functional-relational rather than structural. With due respect to the importance of history, economics as an "explanation" of present events "caused" by events in the past is not admissible. This seems to fit in well with Veblen's insistence on the rọle of genetic process and his impatience with specific causation (economic cause of war). There is much more to be said, but enough has been given to indicate the general drift of organismic theory and its broad kinship with Veblen's point of view.

The question of scope can conveniently be taken up at this point. Veblen was frequently accused of going far outside the realm of economics. Mr. Dorfman intimates that he paid in prestige for this luxury and that an argument used to prevent him from becoming president of the American Economic Association was that the length of his sweep was excessive. In considering scope it is useful to make the somewhat invidious but effective distinction that has recently been made in economic writings between tool-users and tool-makers. From the viewpoint of the mere tool-user, or artisan, it is certain that Veblen exceeded the economists' scope. In fact, it is hardly worth mentioning this except, perhaps, to suggest that some of the criticisms of excessive scope come from persons who have not gone beyond the tool-using stage.

The charge, however, has been brought by tool-makers as well. This is odd, since there is a well-nigh universal professional deformation that inclines the practitioner of any mystery to wish to push his domain out farther and farther. One wonders whether in view of an opposite tendency here some deformation other than the normal professional deformation is not exerting its influence. Whatever the answer, it remains true that scope is purely man-made. The phenomena of nature, of man's relation to nature, and of man's relation to man are not put into separate pigeon holes by a supreme being or by the manner in which the phenomena cluster together. It is only in man's mind that the clustering takes place, and these clusters change as time goes on and knowledge increases. Other sciences do not seem to have this jealous concern about scope. Astronomy cannot be understood or explained without liberal use of physics and chemistry. Physics and chemistry are scarcely distinguishable from each other today, and nuclear chemistry has broken down boundary lines almost completely. Discussions of scope look too much like jurisdictional squabbles between trade unions, bureaucrats, and university deans to have a place in science.

There is little difficulty in evaluating Veblen's iterated and reiterated insistence on the "opaque fact." He performed an obvious service by stimulating descriptive, factual, and quantitative inquiries. Some of his most faithful disciples, in public and private agencies, have set in motion superb machinery for continuing to gather facts and figures. How our ever-more complex economic life would function without them it is difficult to imagine. Admitting their value in practical affairs, one may question their value to institutional theory, which has not advanced in the past quarter century.

Neither can one find fault with Veblen's ability to detach himself from certain important prejudices of the social milieu in which he lived. He is not precisely unusual in this respect, however, and is, in fact, quite run-of-the-mill in substituting a utopian bias for an ideological one—to use Karl Mannheim's [10] phrases. Some readers may feel that here and elsewhere in the text I have not clearly seen the place of ideology and utopia in the "sociology of knowledge" and have misrepresented the views of Mannheim, or of his most competent critics, or both, by speaking invidiously of utopian bias. Some will argue that history would stop if there were no utopians

10 Mannheim, *Ideology and Utopia.*

and their complementing ideologists; some would argue that utopian bias, if it narrows the field of vision, supplies greater light to a more restricted area or enlarges the area that receives less light. All this is speculative; it may even be true, but it has little application to the case in point. We can agree that utopianism is a fine thing, but that Veblen went too far, just as we can agree that French Romanticism was a fine thing without endorsing the excesses of Victor Hugo or Chateaubriand. So much, at least, will be agreed to by reasonable persons.

But this is only the beginning of wisdom. Utopianism may be viewed as a body of knowledge handed down across the centuries, beginning with the lore of primitive magic and ending with the doctrines of modern socialism—a pool of knowledge to which predisposed individuals go for inspiration and to which the competent ones return with contributions. That the existence of such a pool of knowledge about an unreal world has had great value to the real world may be conceded. Excess of utopian bias in an individual is something else. Perhaps a great deal depends on whether the utopian bias is recognized by the owner. It is possible that the bias, to do harm to science, must be an unconscious one—that is, it must disguise itself in various ways and dwell unsuspected in its owner's breast, like unsuspected wishes that lead to undiscovered conflict and push on towards neurosis in individual behavior.

At all events, let us note that any utopia—More's, Morris's, or Gulliver's kingdom of horses—is an aspersive criticism of existing society. The process in reverse is a symptom of utopian bias, and perhaps only Swift and Goya in the Western world have shown more asperity than Veblen in their criticism of existing institutions. Veblen's pejorative words, sadistic literary style, and elaborate castigations brand him as an utopian. They deprive him of the influence he might otherwise have had and of the authority which his theories might have commanded. His social criticism may—like any aesthetic work—have value to other utopians who need a point of identification, but it has no scientific value. His preconception seems to have led him to adopt his fallacious theory of mechanistic psychological determinism and also to have resorted to conjectural history in explaining—or, rather, not explaining—how good and peaceful savages eventually permitted themselves to become despicable barbarians, chained to the bad institutions they had somehow created.

Concerning the neo-Veblenians, I believe it cannot fairly be said that they have an unconscious utopian bias, as Veblen had. On the contrary, most of them consciously aim to improve the world, and with forethought support public proposals similar to those put forward overseas by social democrats or Fabians or the present British Labor Party Government. Most of these proposals favor the working classes and would increase their security or raise their level of living. It is probably safe to say that the neo-Veblenians are pragmatists by choice rather than unconscious utopians. Their interest in the present and the past is primarily to help them shape the future. The light of their knowledge usually focusses upon the possibilities of action, of public control of business, of social and economic planning. It would be brash to say that pragmatism itself suffers from the bias of utopianism, though truth may lie in that direction.

Any final evaluation of utopian bias in institutional theory must take into account the fact that such a bias is more visible among the institutionalists than among standard theorists, precisely because they are *standard*. Our training, in and out of school, through the newspapers, churches, and similar agencies, inhibits us from realizing that competition within civil, criminal, and moral law, the free market, nongovernmental intervention, and the state as umpire—are all utopian goals and unfulfilled aspirations. Reality is seen through the lenses of standard community aims and hopes. Being and seeming and dreaming are so completely intertwined in standard theory that its practitioners do not distinguish among them. Institutional theory, by its insistence on the opaque fact, does succeed in separating, to some degree, what is from what "should" be. Its position on what should be is explicit and therefore of high visibility. Standard theory, appealing as it does to intuition, defends a well-camouflaged Utopia. To the relativist in economic thinking, who changes his post of observation, the camouflage does not conceal the dream-stuff.

But it will be said that there should be no Utopias at all in economics, that the only normal and proper goal of the scientist is to satisfy his idle curiosity. This is a romantic half-truth. It confuses the concept of special goals with general goals. Certainly Roentgen, Becquerel, and the Curies did not work to drop an "atomic" bomb on Hiroshima, August 5, 1945, but they must surely have felt that some further understanding of the relations of matter and energy would be turned to practical use by mankind. The alleged aimlessness of science also confuses personal motives with what might be named social motives. The individual scientist may have no definable goals, but only an uneasy compulsion to pursue certain aimless inquiries. The society which permits him to do this work defines his terms of reference, however, while the schools, or organized professions, or business establishments that provide laboratories, have real, but not always exact, goals in view. Thus, the venturing economic theorist is necessarily preoccupied with the question of goals. In large part, they determine everything he does. The other large part is the economist's theory of human behavior. Without goals and without some concept of the psyche, economists are without the raw materials of their science. It is better to admit that such materials are needed and to examine them with care than to act as if one could proceed from nothing to something.

Let us now go on to the more difficult tasks. We attempt to evaluate the determinism of institutional economics. We must first note that the American scientist normally has no objection to determinism. Possible objections arise only over the identification of the determining forces, their number, the sort of interplay to be discerned among them, and the object to be determined. Most American scholars would probably feel that Veblen reduced too drastically the number of determining forces and that, despite his genuine skill in sensing their interplay, he neglected one kind of reciprocal action, namely, that of the environment on the conscious and controlling mind, and vice versa. This, also, is the basis of differentiation between Veblen and his followers. Neo-Veblenians would concede that certain kinds of special psychological attitudes are determined by vocation, but they would also agree with the criticisms of Veblen's special type of mechanical determinism made in the last chapter.

On another aspect of Veblen's determinism, the congruity-of-culture aspect, the neo-Veblenians do not take a strong position, though, on the whole, they accept it passively. The reader will remember that Veblen seems to assume a sort of nuclear spirit, or dominating force, in each culture, which determines the parts. Can we endorse this as sound methodology? It is certainly in harmony with the psychological concept of the Gestalt and with organismic theory as it has been described above.

In psychology Veblen was not a "configurationist," and, though von Ehrenfels wrote in 1890, thirty-two years before Wertheimer reported early Gestalt experiments, we may safely assume that Veblen stumbled on the concept of a "social Gestalt" independently, or in reading the works of others—perhaps Sombart. Indeed, the Gestalt concept is probably very old and certainly not in disharmony with Hegelianism. The configuration theories are, of course, not accepted by all, though they are recognized as resting on careful study. Even if they were more generally accepted, it would still be open to dispute whether or not one may stretch theories of individual organization to cover social organization. Human beings may be organized wholes and "what happens at one point in the organism is never independent of, or without its influence upon, what is taking place at any other part of the organism." [11] But what is true—or may be true—of a human being is not necessarily true of society.

The concept of a social Gestalt is, however, currently accepted by many sociologists. They think of certain institutions as being appropriate to an agricultural society, for example, and of the persistence of those institutions as being culture lags when they remain virtually unchanged in a nonagricultural, pecuniary, industrial society. Veblen, too, accepted the notion of a culture lag. Despite the necessary congruence of the parts with the whole, exceptions in the form of anachronistic social inheritances were to him admissible exceptions.

In any pattern one must be sure that the incongruities are real, not imaginary—a distinction to which neither Veblen nor his admirers have always paid heed. The dangers of entelechy, teleology, and wishful thinking surround a term such as "cultural lag" and a metaphor like "a horse-and-buggy law in the machine age." How can one decide, for example, whether in this country, the anarchy of state's rights is more appropriate to the machine age than Federal regulation, unless one has some preconceptions about what American life *ought* to be? To say that men must think internationally because engines of destruction become constantly more effective is to assume that man has some destiny other than subjecting himself to self-destruction, which is merely an interesting hypothesis.

Despite spurious congruities and the danger of readily accepting them as real, there do seem to be, in fact, consistent patterns that avoid methodological blunders. It seems unlikely that the Crusades of the eleventh and the twelfth centuries could be re-enacted against the background of contemporary institutions. Could a magnificent frontier "mystique," like that of the United States in the nineteenth century, arise again under the dominating spirit of this age, even if new

[11] R. S. Woodworth, *Contemporary Schools of Psychology*, p. 11.

more clearly noted above, that the determined end, or goal, of Veblenism and that of neo-Veblenism are not the same. Veblen conceives of the virtual and eventual extirpation of conflict and coercion in the economic universe. Here we come unexpectedly on the doctrine that the moral bases must change before human institutions can be substantially improved. The neo-Veblenians are concerned with the immediate attenuation of this conflict or that one and expect a gradual and more complete attenuation of all conflict. Alter the institutions gradually, they say, and let the moral bases of human nature alter gradually with them. Veblen's goal is Utopia—piddling reforms will take care of themselves. Those inspired by his work are reformers, however, some piddling and some not. I do not think it is inconsistent to accept the neo-Veblenians' mild determinism for intermediate goals and Veblen's strict determinism for remote goals. We can probably count on man's intelligence to mitigate somewhat the severity of the business cycle, or the occasional violence of industrial relations, or the abysmal poverty of tropical lands —which is what the neo-Veblenians are striving for now. To Veblen, many of these reforms were merely good housekeeping or an expression of the spirit of business enterprise in a nonreactionary or passably enlightened mood, not the expression of a social will that had unshackled itself from the preconceptions of the business community.

To be sure, the neo-Veblenians are likewise not satisfied with immediate goals or mere housekeeping, but would point out that one goes from a bad stage to a better stage before attaining the best. They seem to hold that the ever-increasing attenuation of coercion may eventually strangle aggression. Such a process of the guttering and final extinction of the flame of conflict is not unlike the process through which, by dint of forcing ourselves to be agreeable to a person whom we dislike we eventually come to be fond of him. No doubt some psychologists would say that such a development fits in with acceptable theories of mental science. Others would be skeptical, holding that some further intervention is required before the aggressive propensities disappear or, sublimated, function constructively in the social interest.

The above discussion has raised many issues, and it is doubtful whether more can profitably be added. I have restated, in terms appropriate to Veblenism and neo-Veblenism, basic questions that have long vexed philosophers and to which no answers have yet been found. No replies can be given where faith alone has jurisdiction. One can only hope that the issues have been stated clearly enough to make easier the task of faith. Let us leave determinism, then, but not until we have noted how Mitchell's response to the questions raised above seems to meet the standards of Veblen and other standards as well. By withdrawing, as he does, from the field of active reform, he avoids the possible errors of the eclectic, reforming pragmatists; by tacit rejection of mechanical determinism, he avoids holding to Veblen's great psychological heresy. By placing faith for a better economic world in psychological discovery, he does not deprive us completely of hope. The further development of psychology is at least a possibility in the current Gestalt, for, despite the limitations placed on idle curiosity by the configuration within which it now operates, the Gestalt does, in fact, permit this unique instinct to discover what does not immediately and narrowly subserve the coercive-pecuniary economy. Thus, Mitchell meets many tests. My only criticism is that he has done very little to stimulate or to help set in motion the kind of psychological discovery that might be useful to economics.

An appraisal of what I have named the hypothetico-deductive method requires many of us to revamp the most solid part of the course in Logic 1 and 2 that formed part of our undergraduate work twenty-five years ago. We must discard the validity of a critically useful distinction between deduction and induction; above all, we must relinquish the Baconian myth that induction is scientific, while deduction is a return to the poverty of fifteenth-century scholasticism or to the sophisms of Gorgias's least honorable followers. We must realize that man's desperate struggle to unveil truth is not governed by the Queensberry rules of induction, but is a catch-as-catch-can affair, in which induction, deduction, inspired insights, lucky accidents, and even seemingly prophetic dreams play their role.

Science has at least two methodological facets: one, proposing solutions to questions; two, verifying proposed solutions with facts. The processes are complementary, and if Veblen's theories are inadequately supported by fact, his defenders may retort that his critics' collections of facts often have no support whatever in theory.

The hypothetico-deductive method finds its chief support among Gestalt theorists. The whole is not only greater than the sum of the parts, but is, in a sense, simpler than the parts and is first perceived. The real issue can perhaps be further clarified by a glance at the actual procedural steps. When a neo-Veblenian decides to study an economic problem he is often influenced by his instrumental or pragmatic and humanitarian bias. He studies monopoly or the distribution of wealth, or the incidence of the social-security tax, or the mechanism for public control of the coal industry. Two bodies of related information are in many cases built up; (1) important basic facts; (2) the appropriate reform or control mechanism. Now, the assumption among neo-Veblenians seems to be that when enough important basic facts from many fields of study are collected, somebody will some day come along to make a "synthesis," that is, will make genuine contributions to institutional theory. There is another assumption, less clearly realized, namely, that the facts being collected for purposes of reform and public control will also be useful for purposes of theory. This, of course, does not follow.

The economist who has theoretical interests primarily works quite differently. Operating under the hypothetico-deductive method, the economist begins with a congruous, useful, and reasonable theory which may or may not make a direct contribution to a reform or humanitarian problem. His investigation searches out the body of facts relevant to his hypothesis, or even only the crucial fact, or the results of a crucial experiment, if one can be devised. The relevant body of facts may not yield either disproof or verification, and the crucial evidence may not be attainable, even after painstaking work and ingenious attempts to set the stage for the critical experiment. In that event the hypothesis will either be abandoned, or, if it works in practice or "fits in" with existing hypotheses of more venerable and honorable parentage, it will be retained. Sketchy and crude though this brief description has been, it does, I trust, adequately support the notion that the amassing of facts by the neo-Veblenians may never—or, at best, only infrequently, or by chance—supply institutional theory with the validating raw material it requires. I think the most that can be said of the monographic material is that the reading or writing of it may put one in the frame of mind to hit upon useful hypotheses.

To give a final opinion on the monographic atomism of the neo-Veblenians is, like evaluation of their psychology, both difficult and easy. Easy, because their conservatism, eclecticism, and agreement with current academic standards make it possible to approve their work as conforming to the sound and tested standards of the day. Difficult, because one scarcely knows how to evaluate methods which, though of great utility in meeting day-to-day problems with day-to-day solutions, make no important theoretical contributions. One is almost tempted to say that most of the conributions to economics made by institutionalists add up to high-grade clerical work and, with Chaucer, to note that "the greatest clerkes ben not the wisest men." Though their techniques be admirable, theoretical progress since Veblen has amounted to very little, or even less. The cautious methods of the neo-Veblenians, however impressive they appear—and in a limited sense they are most impressive, indeed—seem to have the fatal defect of shackling thought—shackling rather than disciplining or inspiring it.

Two matters, one of minor importance, the other of such a speculative character as to warrant only brief treatment, will conclude the substance of this chapter.

Mitchell speaks of the entire alteration of the nature of an economic problem when it is prepared for quantitative rather than nonquantitative treatment.[16] He is wrong if he supposes that only the so-called quantitative method can secure this desirable result. Hoxie's investigation of labor problems, for example, led to quite different results from those that a standard theorist might have secured, yet his study was not statistical. Statistics are but one way to get at opaque facts, and the quantitative method is by no means the only appropriate method. Neither is it the only way in which a traditional problem can be made to alter its aspect.

Also, Veblen talked much—too much, probably—about evolution; but at critical points in the development of his doctrines he gave tacit recognition to dialectical principles rather than to evolutionary principles. The polarity noted in the chapter on psychology—of the instinct of workmanship and its contamination—is a unity of opposites. He also recognizes a "negation of the negation," saying, in effect, that men addicted to business enterprise inevitably bring on a situation in which business enterprise can no longer function. Although the American scientist will have no truck with dialectical processes—and Veblen himself condemned the method of Marx—only a very dogmatic person would say that such processes are completely outside the realm of sound epistemology.[17] Even Wesley Mitchell's self-generating business cycles have a faintly Hegelian odor.

16 See above, p. 63.

17 See D. Struik, review of F. Engel's *Dialektik der Natur*, *Philosophy of Science*, I (1934), 122–123; Haldane, *The Marxist Philosophy and the Sciences*, London, 1938, pp. 30–44; Brown, *Psychology and the Social Order*, pp. 484–486; John Sommerville, *"Dialectical Materialism,"* in *Twentieth Century Philosophy*, ed., by Runes, pp. 471 ff.

It will, perhaps, be said that the word "epistemology" is the key to the errors of this chapter. What is sound epistemology may be bad science. To confuse the two is to expand the sphere of science and to make its field equal to that of philosophy. Perhaps I have allowed science to encroach on faith. But science itself is founded on faith, and there is as much danger in hemming it in between the schoolman's techniques of research as there is in liberating it beyond the bounds of current American practice.

Imagine an intelligent outlander with no knowledge of Western economics or physics—perhaps Montesquieu's Usbek; give him representative books on economics, published in the past few years, and on the physical sciences. He will come to an interesting conclusion: that economists know exactly what they are doing, because their science is old and mature, their methods well-tested, reliable, and simple. Physics, chemistry and astronomy, on the other hand, being new sciences, just emancipated from superstition, are in a chaotic and yeasty state; the practitioners of those mysteries are even ignorant about what is matter and what is energy—one, Mr. Eddington, having invented the inelegant word "wavicle," to express his acknowledged confusion over waves of energy and particles of matter, while another, Mr. Darwin, awkwardly speaks of electrons as being "matter and/or energy." The physicists invoke Plato, Kant, Hegel, Aristotle, and even Comte and Marx to explain what they are trying to do, while they use such words as dialectic, determinism, causality, absolute, like confirmed metaphysicians—and they use "animism" and "teleology" as often as Veblen did. They have been asking themselves such questions as: Why did human beings so long accept without wonder the fact that glass is transparent? Do I really know what time it is—or, at least, what time it is not? Is the law of gravity a law, or is it a manifestation of man's propensity to put himself at the center of the universe?

Despite all this floundering in profundity, they flagellate themselves for being so superficial. Thus, Mr. Zimmer approvingly quotes Mr. Müller on physicists as follows: "We are almost staggered . . . at the idea that so many minds of scientific eminence [in natural science] are unable to look over the fences around their science, and by the fact that the greatest philosophers have lived in vain as far as they are concerned." [18]

Here is a reversal, indeed, since the days of Jeremy Bentham, who sighed that the moral sciences might approach the physical sciences in exactitude. Increasingly astronomers, physicists, and chemists are exhibiting humility and are recognizing that old foes may ride again: egocentrism, intuitive knowledge, animism. Economists, on the other hand, have either no interest in problems of method, assuming them to be of small importance, or have complete confidence in their own methodology, which usually consists of their defective adaptation of method used in the physical sciences.[19] This holds of institutionalism as well as of standard theory.

The greatest recent discovery of science—and this is what relativity suggests—is that the rational eighteenth century and the great nineteenth century did little to abolish superstition and preconception even from the trained scientific mind. Probable error is being reduced day by day; but constant error is slow to reveal itself. The same discovery has been made in psychology. Freud's great contribution is probably a methodological one, similar to the methodological discoveries of physics—namely, that man has a fatal propensity to avoid looking at some of the most important and most clearly visible phenomena of his environment.

[18] A. Muller, *Die philosophischen Grenzfragen der modernen Physik;* quoted by Ernst Zimmer, in *The Revolution in Physics,* New York, Harcourt Brace, n.d., p. 217.

[19] Cf. Joseph Mayer, *Social Science Principles in the Light of Scientific Method,* Durham, N.C., 1941, *passim.*

IV CONCLUSION

ALTHOUGH the institutional variant of general economic theory has added substantially to our understanding of the world we live in, it has disappointed the hopes held for it and is today in a rather seedy state. Veblen got institutional economics off to a bad start, in this country, at least, with his social satire, literary sadism, and difficult style. He attracted men of genuine stature, but he also attracted inconsequential rebels, nonconformists, reformers, and dissenters. Mitchell followed with occasional essays on fundamental issues, which have nourished theory only enough to keep it in a state of suspended animation; his interests lay elsewhere. During the 1930's and 1940's the competent younger men have become absorbed in the great problems of the day, which are being met in a political atmosphere that is not uncongenial to their preconceptions. They have elaborated a practical program which is related to Veblenism by cousinhood rather than paternity. Finally, Keynes has lent good repute to a program of action that is at least partly congruous with the neo-Veblenian program of action. Keynes has, therefore, deflected towards himself the forces of attraction that might otherwise have moved directly towards Veblen. Thus, the accidents of personalities and events seem to explain why institutional economics is run down at the heels.

But the search for explanations can be conducted on a deeper level. Despite certain areas of agreement between Veblen and neo-Veblenians—such as emphasis on conflict and disorganization, dissatisfaction with standard theory, the need to discover the "opaque facts"—there are great differences.

Veblen had a philosophical, European, nineteenth-century mind; those under his inspiration are less Veblenians than they are twentieth-century North Americans, empirical, eclectic, pragmatic, often subscribing even to a debased pragmatism. Impatient with the Hegelianism of Marx and the hedonism of standard theory, they have sought to skirt error by avoiding any consciously-made philosophical assumptions. But this in itself leads to an assumption, and because the assumption is unconsciously made or accepted with light heart, it is a dangerous preconception. What assumption? That naïve induction, eclecticism, empiricism, pragmatism, sacred or profane, can be fruitful. This too is philosophical and may lead nowhere even more surely than does faith in neo-Hegelianism or the viewpoints inspired by Gestalt psychology or Freud. The point to be made is that mankind is not willing to stay within the limits of knowledge set by his tools of observation, and this is necessarily more nearly true of the social sciences, where the tools are few and crude, than in the physical sciences, where they are many and delicate—or powerful. Since the mind does, in fact, fill up the gaps, let us make sure that the filling of gaps is done on the basis of conscious, adult decisions, not on the basis of the unconscious and unremembered fears and hopes of childhood, or the biases with which all men are endowed by their Creator and their institutions.

Since there has been no adequate philosophy among economists, there has been no adequate psychology, because without a definite philosophy there is no need for a definite psychology. Indeed, there has been no genuine exploration of psychology by those who most earnestly desire to bring new concepts of human nature to the service of economic theory.

With these considerations in mind, I would say that the under-development of institutional theory results from a cause that Veblen himself foresaw (though he would have expressed it differently), namely, the extreme difficulty that even the strongest human propensities have of transcending the Gestalt in which they find themselves. In other words, the "instinct of idle curiosity," though occasionally competent enough and strong enough to escape from its environment, is normally bound down by the institutions in which it operates. The attitudes engendered by the monetary-coercive-machine economy have, according to plan, converted the vigorous "evolutionary economics" of Veblen into a degraded form of pragmatism, eclectic, empirical, uncertain, opportunistic.

What can the economist do to get out of this situation, and how can idle curiosity be strengthened to restore vigor to institutional thought? I wish I were able to give an answer that would inform and inspire my neo-Veblenian colleagues, but I have had no more success in transcending the Gestalt than they. If, however, the reader is willing to consider a few suggestions offered only in the subjunctive mood, I shall venture to put them down.

First of all, the world cannot afford to lose the journeyman economist, whether as civil servant or private citizen; neither will the economist gain by withdrawing from the world of affairs and taking to his tower of ivory. Proposed social and economic legislation must be scrutinized, its repercussions foreseen, and, if adopted, its results observed, analyzed, and recorded. Only economists are competent to do such jobs—the thousand and one jobs of rural, urban, state, and national housekeeping. With all their faults, they are the only persons sufficiently divorced from the special interests of the ironmonger, hog-grower, truck-driver, or brush salesman to be able to see, as Marshall put it, "the one in the many and the many in the one." The world would fall apart if these artisan services were withdrawn, and theory would become sterile if theorists had no contact with reality.

The master economist must, however, view his mystery from a higher ground than that on which the artisan stands. To reach this higher level one requirement is frank dealing with the subject of aggression. Economists who are now only half willing to use the underlying concept of human conflict must make up their minds. If they feel they must discard it, well and good. They will develop theories in harmony with that decision. If they decide to use it, then they must use it consciously, and with understanding. Coercion must be thought of as a generalized form of behavior, not as the peculiar possession of an elite, whether it be business enterprisers or business-union leaders. It is only in this way that indignation can be dissolved and the concept of aggression become fruitful. The economist, if he makes coercion the center of his universe, must learn to take the same attitude towards it as does the practicing psychoanalyst, who has virtually freed himself of valuative attitudes in this domain of behavior. When we come honestly to believe that it is a normal component of human action, used wherever and however institutionally permitted, and elsewhere either harmfully repressed or usefully sublimated—when we begin to look upon it in this fashion, we shall be freed from moral attitudes that now inhibit full use of the principle of aggression in economic analysis. Acceptance of such a view is hard. It can easily lead to cynicism, which also inhibits freedom of thought. It concedes that those already strong enjoy "unfair" advantages, but it recognizes that the weak, too, can fight back, as Simmel has noted. And, finally, it makes us observe that weak and strong, and weak and weak, and strong and strong are caught up in an endlessly aggressive process that can lead only to continued aggression and a denial of the hopes of the constructive propensities.

The institutionalist must familiarize himself with psychology. He has succeeded long enough, with a minimum basis, in sustaining a maximum bluff. He must know enough to be original in psychology, when necessary, blending, synthesizing, and selecting—enough to bend the theories of mental science to serve economic science. The institutionalist's ignorant faith—I know my phrases are strong—in something he names "behaviorism" simply will not do much longer.

Institutionalism should undertake two immediate short-run tasks. One is to rewrite Veblen understandably with the benefits of contemporary insights and vocabulary. The job I have in mind is a process of writing-over, not unlike the re-writing of Ricardo done by a long line of classical economists. Veblen deserves his John Stuart Mill. A sympathetic rewriting, amputation of bootless social criticism, modernization, correction of minor errors, filling-in of gaps, and putting into one volume would give the world a better chance to see what has been done, what is worthy of more attention, what the fundamental weaknesses of the institutional approach are.

The other immediate task is to attempt to write a comprehensive treatise on money. Though money is the nucleus of institutional theory, surprisingly little has been written on the subject, and that little is of minor importance, or, if important, negative. If money is a weapon of coercion, we ought to know more about how men wield that weapon. In a general way we know what redistributions of wealth take place under inflation and deflation; we know how currencies can be depreciated to serve international conflicts over the control of foreign markets; we have Simmel's interesting approach to monetary problems. But nobody has put all this together between two covers; it seems a particularly appropriate job for an institutionalist.

None of the jobs just suggested—even if done well—would do much to push knowledge farther. But they would confer the same benefits on economic theory that stock-taking and budget-making confer on business enterprises. They would, besides, give scattered persons who think alike something to rally around, to work with, to confirm or to reject. They might lead to the creation of a Journal of Institutional Economics—perhaps a doubtful boon to science, yet a center of attraction whose advantages should at least be explored. There might even be a National Bureau of Research in Institutional Economics, Inc., with a directorate composed of associated philosophers, economists, and psychologists.

Perhaps the most direct way of attaining higher ground is to cultivate the mood of reaching towards absolutes. Though two-thirds of the world's inhabitants are directly concerned with agriculture, economic study is still centered on city men or, at least, on the nations having advanced industrial development. Economics is based on physics, geography, biology, psychology. We must square our work with the conclusions of those sciences and then with the world as a total entity before we can put forward a single hypothesis. I am thinking of the global scope and thought-boldness of the geopolitical thinkers—Ratzel, Mackinder, Haushofer—and wondering why their world-embracing view does not come easily to those who would place their abilities at the service of the constructive instincts.

Somewhere along the road the economist will have to think about final goals—about his utopia, in short, and how to get there. Do we creep up on utopia by slow, painful steps, or do we make saltatory progress? Do we need to burst a Gestalt before we can make appreciable changes in it? Can we rely on changing institutions to change human nature, or must man first be changed, or must both processes go along together? Does the moral basis of the good society precede the institutional? Is general, mutual and reciprocal coercion the chief obstacle to abundant economic productivity and the achievement of better levels of living for all?

The evolution of the world during the past quarter century has created a difficult situation for those who seek the vaster generalizations. Within a recent fortnight the United Kingdom voted in an overwhelmingly strong labor government, New Mexico was the scene of a great initial experiment that released atomic energy for practical use, while three men in Potsdam were determining the calculable future of Europe. For much of the world economic decisions are not being left and will not be left to the impersonal forces of economic competition and devil-take-the-hindmost, but to the conscious decision of identifiable individuals. It is astonishing to think that whether these millions of people shall starve or those millions of people shall eat, is not being decided by the negative and impersonal policies of drift and nonintervention, but by the positive policies of a relatively few persons, many of whom could be named. It is amazing to think that during the past five years in every part of the world such issues as whether shoestrings or mandolin strings shall be produced, have been decided by definite persons, commissioned to do exactly that, and it is equally astonishing to realize that for a large part of the world such decisions will continue to be made by namable individuals. Communism is no longer an abstraction, to be examined with classroom objectivity and then thrown away each year at the end of the first course on economics. It is a force on the march, a force that scarcely resembles the construct of an earlier day. Wars and the fear of wars, political overturns and the fear of them, will do as much to determine economic activity as any purely economic aims or decisions—though one cannot deny the reciprocal effect of economic evolution on political considerations.

This is the day of flying box-cars shod with tires distilled from dandelion wine, of trade unionism in politics, national and international, of civilian slaughter in warfare, of rockets and radar and televising and stratospherical flight, of industrial revolutions in tropical countries. All these phenomena and much else besides must be seen together if we can expect to develop a useful economic theory, free from egocentrism, of the relative view, and tending instead towards general validity.

Those who may be moved to follow the suggestions made above will probably find themselves withdrawing from the trend of contemporary American scholarship, not only from the trend in economics but also in many of the other sciences. This may invite solitude and occasionally arouse a sense of discouragement, but departure from contemporary practice would not, alone, prevent achievement of the highest order.

These are troubled days, and there is nothing to indicate that we shall be spared serious social disorganization. We may soon find ourselves closer to barbarism than we are now, with our democratic freedom of inquiry forgotten. We cannot, of course, order our lives to conform to a vague and distant threat or to a Veblenian prediction; but our possibly impending fate may make us think that man's responsibility today—like that of the frog in a bowl of milk, who, without plan but with optimistic vigor, thrashed up a safe island of butter—that man's current responsibility is to act, not to theorize. Well, perhaps it is. On the other hand, most of the great hypotheses of mankind seem to make contact with everyday life by roundabout ways and to impose remote or even paradoxical rather than direct manipulation. We send messages rapidly, not by training fast-running couriers, but by letting loose immaterial impulses. We cool our rooms, not by conserving better last winter's ice, but by compressing gases and letting them expand—something that permits use of fire to produce cold. Doors open in front of us because a beam of light beside us is intercepted. Great statesmen become familiar to us because certain processes result in the emission of sound and light waves that nearly duplicate the waves emitted or reflected by the right honorable gentlemen themselves. In a world like this, the way of achieving a more effective economic organization may be suggested by studies that have little to do with the coal industry, or cartels, or social security, or business cycles, or trade unions. Perhaps psychology holds the key to the mystery of economics.

In the meantime, the sun never sets on unattenuated violence, and the ends we think we seek are denied by the methods we use. The evidence for an early peaceable civilization "is circumstantial" today, as it was when Veblen used the same phrase in a similar context. This, however, should not make us despair, for it is quite possible that human behavior when it changes, does not change by the slow accretions of an evolutionary process, but changes rapidly by a dialectic process. The constructive propensities are strong, and the fact that they are now placed primarily at the service of the family does not mean that they cannot ultimately be made available to larger social groups. What is important today is that in the waging of war and the building of peace, the resulting economic and political systems shall tolerate freedom of inquiry. If idle curiosity can operate in an atmosphere of freedom for a few more decades, everything dear to man's utopian bias may yet be won.

SELECTED BIBLIOGRAPHY

Anderson, Karl L. "The Unity of Veblen's Theoretical System," *Quarterly Journal of Economics,* XLVII, No. 4 (Aug., 1933), 598–626. Probably the best short article on Veblen's theories.

Ayres, C. E. The Theory of Economic Progress. Chapel Hill, Univ. of North Carolina, 1944. A good example of contemporary neo-Veblenian writing.

Bridgman, Percy W. The Logic of Modern Physics. New York, Macmillan, 1927.

—— Nature of Physical Theory, Princeton, Princeton Univ. Press, 1936.

—— The Intelligent Individual and Society. New York, Macmillan, 1938.

These books by a distinguished physicist express his views on scientific methodology. One of his reviewers stated that the second book listed above apparently puts him in the camp of the Bergsonians.

Brown, J. F. Psychology and the Social Order. New York, McGraw-Hill, 1936.

An impressive, exciting book, though of uneven merit. Contains in Part I, particularly in Chapter II and in Appendix A, a most provocative contribution to methodology in the social sciences—namely, the "field-theoretical approach." A comprehensive scheme of social psychology rooted in the theories of Gestalt psychology. Excellent summary and critique of Freud's theories, pp. 308–328.

Clark, John M. Preface to Social Economics; Essays on Economic Theory and Social Problems. New York, Farrar & Rinehart, 1936.

A collection of essays; several writers have listed J. M. Clark among the institutionalists. This book has a fine essay on Mitchell, pp. 390–416, which includes an interesting exchange of letters between the two men. See also the essay on economics and psychology, pp. 92–170. The introduction to the book by Moses Abramovitz and Eli Ginzberg is excellent. W. C. Mitchell has indicated the great usefulness to institutional theory of Clark's *Studies in the Economics of Overhead Costs,* Chicago, University of Chicago Press, 1923.

Dorfman, Joseph. Thorstein Veblen and His America. New York, Viking, 1934.

The biography and the milieu; definitive. Contains excellent summaries of Veblen's books; a Veblenian bibliography goes back to 1884.

Einstein, Albert, and Sigmund Freud. Why War? Paris, International Institute of Intellectual Co-operation (League of Nations), 1933.

Freud's letter to Einstein in this little volume is, considering its brevity, the most useful of Freud's writings for the purposes of institutional psychology.

Feigl, Herbert. "Logical Empiricism," in Twentieth Century Philosophy, ed. by Runes. New York, Philosophical Library, 1943.

A logical empiricist (logical positivist of the Vienna Circle), the author of this article supports the same general type of organismic theory that has claimed the support of B. F. Brown (see Brown, above, and pp. 67, 68 of this book).

Freud, Sigmund. A General Introduction to Psycho-Analysis. Revised. New York, Liveright, 1935.

An early book, to some degree superseded by his later work. See above, Einstein and Freud.

—— New Introductory Lectures on Psycho-Analysis. New York, Norton, 1933.

The last half of Chapter IV discusses the polarity of the constructive-destructive instinct, on which so much of my analysis of Veblen is based. The last few pages of the *Lectures* contain an interesting discussion of Marx and the USSR. Like Veblen, Freud taxes Marx for his neo-Hegelianism (p. 242). Freud is hard reading for any but serious students. Menninger (below) is easier and for our limited purposes, just as good.

Gruchy, Allan G. "The Concept of National Planning in Institutional Economics," *Southern Economic Journal,* VI (Oct., 1939), pp. 121–144.

—— "The Economics of the National Resources Committee," *American Economic Review,* XXIX (March, 1939), 60–73.

—— "John R. Commons' Concept of Twentieth-Century Economics," *Journal of Political Economy,* XLVIII (Dec., 1940), 823–849.

These useful articles offer a panoramic view of neo-institutional activities and concerns in recent years.

Haldane, J. B. S. The Marxist Philosophy and the Sciences. London, Allen and Unwin, 1938.

A study by a distinguished British scientist of the relationship between the methodology and content of science, on the one hand, and Marxist principles on the other. Haldane finds many similarities and some identities.

Hamilton, W. H. "The Development of Hoxie's Economics," *Journal of Political Economy,* XXIX (1916), 855–883.

This bargain-counter item offers two distinguished American institutional economists for the price of one: Hamilton, the author; Hoxie, the subject. Other books by Hamilton are: *Pattern of Competition,* (New York, Columbia University Press, 1940); *The Control of Wages* (with Stacy May), New York, Doran, 1923. For Hoxie, see below.

Harris, Abram L. "Types of Institutionalism," *Journal of Political Economy,* XL (Dec., 1932), 721–750.

A comparison of the methods used and the goals sought by Marx, Veblen, and W. C. Mitchell.

Homan, Paul T. Contemporary Economic Thought. New York, Harper, 1928.

One essay in this book is given over to Veblen, another to Mitchell. Written nearly twenty years ago, both essays are still most valuable critiques.

Hoxie, Robert F. Trade Unionism in the United States. 2d ed. New York, Appleton, 1931.

A book by one of Veblen's three outstanding "pupils," in Veblen's own estimation, the two others being W. C. Mitchell and H. J. Davenport. This book and the earlier essays on which it is based have had a strong influence on all subsequent work in this field and demonstrate how one may relentlessly pursue the "opaque fact" without benefit of statistics.

Keynes, J. M. The General Theory of Employment, Interest and Money. New York, Harcourt Brace, 1936.

No book published in the field of economics during the past quarter century, at least, has created a greater stir than this one. It is an important public document in the sense that current demands for full employment and expanding production find theoretical justification here.

Mannheim, Karl. Ideology and Utopia. New York, Harcourt Brace, 1936.

In this study of the "sociology of knowledge" the problems of the observer, who has a personal interest in social and economic outcomes, are discussed with great insight.

Menninger, Karl, and J. L. Menninger. Love against Hate. New York, Harcourt Brace, 1942.

An easy-to-read book based on Freudian doctrines, though only incidentally a summary of them, the author's intention being to supply a guide to the everyday psychological problems of normal life. Despite its popular style, original material is presented. Interesting discussions of the polarity and sublimation of the constructive (love) propensities and the destructive (hate) ones, will be found on pp. 129–133; 163; 295–296.

Mitchell, Wesley C. The Backward Art of Spending Money and Other Essays. New York, McGraw-Hill, 1937.

These collected essays, lectures, and reviews cover a period of twenty-five years and represent Mitchell's nonquantitative work. There are interesting essays on Veblen, Sombart, Commons, three great institutionalists. The essay on Bentham is, in a sense, an essay on institutional psychology.

—— Business Cycles; the Problem and Its Setting. New York, National Bureau of Economic Research, Inc., 1927.

Of all institutionalist writings, Chapter II of this book, pp. 61–186, comes nearest to being a Principles of Institutional Economics. Homan's *Contemporary Economic Thought* contains a good summary of an earlier (1913) and cruder, but similar book on the same subject, pp. 391–410. Better than Homan on this, partly because written after the publication of Mitchell's 1927 book, is J. M. Clark's essay (see above).

Osborn, R., *pseud.* (Reuben Osbert). Freud and Marx: a Dialectical Study. New York, Equinox, 1937.

A demonstration to Marxists that Freud is no heretic; an interesting, but not always convincing, book on similarities between Freud and Marx.

Tawney, R. H. The Acquisitive Society, New York, Harcourt Brace, 1920.

A book widely read by American radicals and "liberals" at the time of publication. His notions of "acquisitive" and "functional" recall Veblen's correlative "pecuniary" and "industrial."

Veblen, Thorstein V. Absentee Ownership. New York, Huebsch, 1923.

The treatment of American economic history in this book is, perhaps, as systematic as his treatment of economic theory in the *Theory of Business Enterprise*. The history that forms part of the book, like that of the supplementary notes in *Imperial Germany*, is, however, incidental to another thesis—in this case to the nature of large-scale banking. Summary in Dorfman's *Thorstein Veblen*, pp. 467–485.

—— The Instinct of Workmanship and the State of the Industrial Arts. New York, Macmillan, 1914.

The basic Veblenian book, containing the eggs from which most of the others seem to have hatched. Veblen himself declared it to be his only important work. Summaries may be found in Karl L. Anderson's article listed above, Dorfman's *Thorstein Veblen*, pp. 324–329, and Homan's *Contemporary Economic Thought*, pp. 128–151.

—— The Place of Science in Modern Civilization and Other Essays. New York, Huebsch, 1919.

A selection of Veblen's earlier essays brought together by his friends and published in book form. The first six essays contain his most important formal methodological work. This important group, as such, is summarized in Dorfman's *Thorstein Veblen*, pp. 155–164; the remaining essays in the collection Dorfman summarizes under the title of the individual essay, not under the name of the book.

—— The Theory of Business Enterprise. New York, Scribner's, 1904.

Generally considered to be Veblen's nearest approach to a general work on economic theory, strictly speaking. Summaries of this book may be found in Dorfman's *Thorstein Veblen*, pp. 225–235, and in Homan's *Contemporary Economic Thought*, pp. 151–162.

—— The Theory of the Leisure Class: an Economic Study of the Evolution of Institutions. New York, Macmillan, 1899.

Has been reprinted inexpensively: Vanguard; Modern Library. The first book published by Veblen and usually the book to which those desiring to make his acquaintance are first referred. More playful and of more general interest than his other books. This is where the famous phrases "conspicuous leisure" and "conspicuous consumption" come from. A summary may be found in Dorfman's *Thorstein Veblen*, pp. 174–191. The facts that this is the Veblenian primer and that it is sometimes hilariously funny should not blind the reader to its importance.

—— What Veblen Taught. New York, Viking, 1936.

Obviously not a book by Veblen in the usual sense, but a volume of his writings, selected by and with an introduction by Wesley Mitchell. Not (like *Place of Science*) a bringing together of single and scattered articles, but an anthology, selected with the idea of giving, in brief compass Veblen's basic ideas. Probably the most valuable single book to own.

Veblen wrote well over one hundred articles, books, and reviews. They are listed and identified in Joseph Dorfman's *Thorstein Veblen and His America,* pp. 519–524. It is not necessary to list them here. Above I call attention to the books that are most relevant to my analysis. Dorfman does a fine job of summarizing briefly, yet completely, the argument of each of Veblen's major works. Veblen's books have been reprinted from time to time; I have given original dates of publication and original publishers.

INDEX